**SOMERSET MUSIC
EDUCATION PROGRAMME**

Growing with Music:
KEY STAGE 1
☆
Teacher's Book

Michael Stocks and Andrew Maddocks

LONGMAN

Acknowledgements

The Somerset Music Education Programme started because many local primary teachers and Heads believed in the educational benefits to be gained from including music within the day to day curriculum of the primary school – and were prepared to give time and effort to the improvement of their own music and teaching skills. As a result, through singing and aural activity reinforced by movement and instrument work, many children in Somerset primary schools have grown in musical confidence and awareness. It is an evolutionary process in which we learn from each other. Sandra Oldfield and Elizabeth Bates, Somerset's Primary Support Teachers for Music, have helped us in the preparation of the written material, proposing ideas and much practical guidance from their own teaching experience. We are also grateful to Susan Young for contributing with such understanding to those aspects of the project which relate to movement.

We should have made little progress if we had not also tried to benefit from the experience of distinguished music teachers and writers on music education from previous generations: to mention a few, we wish to acknowledge our debt to the work and writings of John Curwen; to the collections and observations of Cecil Sharp and Percy Grainger; to Bernarr Rainbow's research into the history of music education in Britain; and to Zoltán Kodály. The Somerset project owes much to the music education practice in Hungary which grew out of Kodály's insight and leadership and the work of his students and disciples, so many of whom are now distinguished teachers and music educators of international standing and influence. To our Hungarian friends in particular, therefore, and to those many acquaintances in North America who share our admiration of the Hungarian example – our grateful thanks.

Finally, we should like to acknowledge our gratitude to the Winston Churchill Memorial Trust for making possible study visits to Hungary and the United States of America, and to the contribution of the Calouste Gulbenkian Foundation, without whose support (along with that of Somerset County Council) the preparation of draft materials, their trials in Somerset schools and their dissemination beyond Somerset would not have been possible.

Michael Stocks   **Andrew Maddocks**
Adviser for Music   Advisory Teacher for Music

(Somerset Education Department)

Contents

Somerset Music Education Programme: the components

Key Stage 1

Teacher's Book 1	0 582 03937 1
Cassette 1	0 582 03936 3
The Key Stage 1 Evaluation Pack (Teacher's Book and Cassette)	0 582 09750 9

Key Stage 2A

Teacher's Book 2A	0 582 03944 4
Cassette 2A	0 582 03942 8
Pupil's Book 1	0 582 03947 9
Pupil's Book 2	0 582 03946 0
The Key Stage 2A Evaluation Pack (Teacher's Book 2A; Pupil's Books 1 & 2; Cassette)	0 582 09751 7

Key Stage 2B

Teacher's Book 2B	0 582 03943 6
Cassette 2B	0 582 03941 X
Pupil's Book 3	0 582 03945 2
Pupil's Book 4	0 582 03948 7
The Key Stage 2B Evaluation Pack (Teacher's Book 2B; Pupil's Books 3 & 4; Cassette 2B)	0 582 09752 5

Introduction

Somerset Music Education Programme

Primary phase: the programme's purpose and context

This programme is the result of well-tried practice in Somerset primary schools over a six-year period. Essentially, it aims to develop the musicianship of children across the whole of the primary age range by increasing aural awareness, encouraging 'inner ear' response and enabling musical thinking. It is concerned with those elements of music which are common to all musical styles – whether the music be, for example, English folk song, American musicals, or the classical music of North India.

We are born with two ears and one voice. Throughout life these are the human faculties most necessary for communication. Their development is essential to our well-being and to the quality of our intellectual, physical and spiritual growth. Yet, surprisingly, we do little consciously to develop them. In school, year after year, we are failing to recognise their remarkable educational potential – in music, a potential which is only realised (as with 'mother-tongue' in language) by a constant use of the singing voice and the development of the inner ear.

Most people would agree that music is to be enjoyed and, sensibly, the word 'enjoyment' is often to be seen in the school's music syllabus. As teachers, however, we should remember that enjoyment is a wide-ranging emotion – on the one hand associated with fun and laughter, on the other with that deep satisfaction which comes only from achievement. In education there is, of course, a place for both; but if we are to justify a place for music in the school curriculum beyond its present largely recreational status, we need to ensure that its joys and demands play a full part in the education of all children from their first days in school, and that the necessary preparations are made to guarantee for every child the progressive accumulation of skill, experience and insight necessary for musical achievement and independence.

This programme, then, offers to the teacher (both 'non-specialist' and 'specialist') a structure upon which a music curriculum can be based. It is not a method, but it does contain a sequence designed to help bring about a process of learning. It makes substantial use of the voice, but at the same time recognises the value of movement and instruments. It does not set out to tell you, the teacher, what to do – because nothing can replace your teaching or be a substitute for it, and the quality of child response will always depend upon your attitudes and expectations as a teacher. You need to be convinced in your own mind that your aims and objectives are both reasonable and appropriately demanding. Your commitment and enthusiasm will then communicate readily to your class – more than compensating for any lack of experience you may feel in the early stages, or any anxiety about your level of musical skill.

However, a child's education must have progression, continuity and achievement. Therefore, within the overall pattern of class activity, structure your teaching to allow for the frequent practice of skills and for the application and sharing of acquired knowledge. Work to your strengths – and, having made a start, seek out local music and in-service training opportunities to help improve your personal music skills, confidence and imagination. Most of all, enjoy making music with your children.

A welcome to the 'non-specialist' teacher

The Somerset Music Education Programme denies the view that musical 'giftedness' is a prerequisite of musical development; it also denies that musical 'giftedness' is a prerequisite for teaching music. Yet the tradition dies hard, fuelled by the common expectation of generations – that in order to include music in your primary curriculum it is necessary, for example, to be able to play the piano.

The Somerset Music Education Programme proposes that music should occupy a place within the day to day activities of the primary school class, as a part of normal curriculum entitlement, and suggests ways in which this might be achieved. It builds on the belief (now borne out in practice) that most primary teachers, given appropriate resources and a little support, can do a great deal to help their children acquire basic music skills and experience – so that the children are enabled to use music in practical situations and thus to grow in personal confidence and self-esteem.

The Somerset Music Education Programme was initially devised, therefore, with primary children and their class teachers in mind. Since its introduction into schools, hundreds of Somerset teachers have used and appraised the written materials. Over a period of six years considerable revisions were made on the basis of teachers' observations and suggestions. Not surprisingly, these teachers possessed a wide range of personal music experience, skill and confidence, but it has been gratifying to make the following discoveries:

1 The inexperienced teacher discovered a course with a structure which clearly defines musical goals, concepts and skills, and which shows how these can be acquired and achieved in the context of the primary class.

2 Those lacking initial confidence discovered a programme with a supportive framework, offering appropriate and relevant songs, cassettes to help the teacher learn the songs, a wide choice of teaching ideas and plenty of clear guidance for 'getting started'.

3 Experienced teachers discovered a resource which helped to increase their teaching effectiveness, to strengthen their resolve and to supply, in a comprehensive form, new teaching material and ideas.

The Somerset Music Education Programme is a valuable resource for schools reviewing their teaching approaches to conform to the requirements of the National Curriculum. It offers a firm skill/concept base which, once established, enables perceptive teachers (not just the so-called 'specialists') to move forward imaginatively in ways which are relevant to their children and to local circumstances.

The Somerset Music Education Programme is comprised of materials which make up a series, as follows:

GROWING WITH MUSIC: Key Stage 1 (Age 4–7 years)
Written with the so-called 'non-specialist' teacher in mind, this stage suggests ideas for increasing the musical awareness of younger children by listening, singing, movement and playing.

GROWING WITH MUSIC: Key Stage 2A (Age 7–9 years)
Intended for junior 'starters', this is also a continuation programme for those who began with *Growing with Music: Key Stage 1*. The repertoire is chosen for older children, of course, and written material for the use of the children is included.

GROWING WITH MUSIC: Key Stage 2B (Age 9–11 years)
This is a continuation programme for those seeking to move on from *Growing with Music: Key Stage 2A*.

Assessment of the music curriculum

Recent curriculum reform in all countries of the United Kingdom requires that assessment is an integral part of the educational process – by informing curriculum planning, by making possible the recording of individual pupil progress and by supporting the evaluation of teaching performance. The outcomes of these reforms are expressed in different ways for England, Northern Ireland, Scotland and Wales because each country has reviewed the curriculum within its own context and terms of reference. The result is a rich tapestry of experience which makes rewarding reading for all teachers. The 'Growing with Music' programme relates strongly to the music curriculum objectives expressed in each of the four countries, as shown in the Appendix to this book which contains charts connecting 'Growing with Music' to each country's Programmes of Study.

Assessment has been an integral part of the preparation of the 'Growing with Music' programme. The Skill/Concept index (page 19) is in itself a powerful support for assessment, but probably too detailed for most teachers to use as a basis for reasonable assessment procedures. Consequently, Record of Assessment sheets are provided at the end of this Teacher's Book (see *Copymasters*, pages 203–214) for schools in England, Northern Ireland, Scotland and Wales, based upon the End of Key Stage Statements (or equivalent) for each country. It is for the teacher to decide, in accordance with his/her assessment practice in other curriculum areas or with assessment systems already in place in the school, whether the assessment criteria columns should contain a tick, a felt-tipped pen colour-coded mark, a graded mark or a reference to a written descriptive judgement elsewhere.

Music Curriculum Assessment (England)

National Curriculum documentation makes it clear that assessment arrangements for music will not include nationally prescribed tests and, in consequence, concludes that assessment of achievement in music will for most pupils be by teachers only. It further recommends that assessment be made against the End of Key Stage Statements. It also says that assessment should be simple and part of the classroom process, thus making only reasonable demands on time.

In this programme two assessments are proposed for Key Stage 1, and four assessments for Key Stage

2 – an annual record of pupil progress by criterion statements under the two attainment targets of Performing/Composing and Listening/Appraising.

Record of Assessment sheets for Key Stage 1 (England) are provided as Copymasters (pages 203–4). The 'Name' column is for the names of the pupils to be listed. The 'Comments' column is for the teacher to make observations about individual pupils, particularly to inform reports to parents. The narrow columns in the middle relate to the assessment criteria which appear under the Attainment Targets 'Performing/Composing' and 'Listening/Appraising'.

Music Curriculum Assessment (Northern Ireland)

The Northern Ireland Curriculum: Music states that 'as music will not be the subject of compulsory assessment the statements of attainment contained in the document are included for the guidance of teachers only . . . (they) do not form part of the statutory provisions'.

The Record of Assessment sheets in this Programme relate to Levels 1–5, resulting in a record of pupil progress by statements of attainment under the two Attainment Targets of 'Making Music' and 'Responding to Music with understanding'. Although non-statutory, they are a very useful guide to assessment criteria.

Record of Assessment sheets for Levels 1–3 (Northern Ireland) are provided as Copymasters (pages 205–210). The 'Name' column is for the names of the pupils to be listed. The 'Comments' column is for the teacher to make observations about individual pupils, particularly to inform reports to parents. The narrow columns in the middle relate to the statements of attainment which appear under the Attainment Targets.

Music Curriculum Assessment (Scotland)

Record of Assessment sheets for Level A (Scotland) are provided as Copymasters (pages 211–212) at the end of this Teacher's Book. The 'Name' column is for the names of the pupils to be listed. The 'Comments' column is for the teacher to make observations about individual pupils, particularly to inform reports to parents. The narrow columns in the middle are aligned to the assessment criteria which relate to the Attainment Targets within the three common outcomes. The assessment criteria are 'concerned with pupils' abilities to:

- select, control and use media, technique, skills etc. appropriate to the task;

- generate, investigate and communicate their own ideas and show that they can develop and sustain them in a variety of ways;

- describe significant features of their own and others' work and make informed judgements and choices.'

The Record of Assessment sheets assume an annual assessment. The sheets labelled 'First Assessment' contain assessment criteria related to the 'Growing with Music' Programme which are also in line with the Attainment Targets. Sheets labelled 'Attainment Targets' are the final sheets at each Level. The full text of each attainment target is to be found in *Expressive Arts 5–14*.

Music Curriculum Assessment (Wales)

National Curriculum documentation makes it clear that assessment arrangements for music will not include nationally prescribed tests and, in consequence, concludes that assessments of achievement in music will for most pupils be by teachers only. It further recommends that assessments be made against the End of Key Stage Statements. It also says that assessment should be simple and part of the classroom process, thus making only reasonable demands on time.

In this programme, two assessments are proposed for Key Stage 1, and four assessments for Key Stage 2 – an annual record of pupil progress by criterion statements under the three attainment targets of Performing, Composing and Appraising.

Record of Assessment sheets for Key Stage 1 (Wales) are provided as Copymasters (pages 213–214) at the end of this Teacher's Book. The 'Name' column is for the names of the pupils to be listed. The 'Comments' column is for the teacher to make observations about individual pupils, particularly to inform reports to parents. The narrow columns in the middle relate to the assessment criteria which appear under the Attainment Targets 'Performing, Composing and Appraising'.

The Key Stage 1 Course

The Child

1 *Growing with Music: Key Stage 1* gives children aged 4–7 years a programme of music education, the structure of which is founded upon musical experience and the ways in which children learn.

2 The child is central to the learning structure. *Growing with Music: Key Stage 1* principally seeks to stimulate and develop the child's musicality. In particular, it is the intention of this educational programme that each child, as appropriate to his/her stage of vocal, intellectual and emotional development, will:

   a learn a collection of songs which have musical merit;

   b discover his/her singing voice, and sing with quality;

   c develop an accurate and discriminatory aural sense;

   d develop the facility known as aural thinking (audiating);

   e develop the motor skills of the body so that rhythmic and melodic concepts in music can be experienced through movement;

   f develop a kinaesthetic memory – i.e. an association between the music and physical movement;

   g develop the basic manipulative skills for playing certain instruments;

   h develop with increasing fluency the ability to read music notation;

   i develop an ability to sing and write music from memory;

   j develop a facility for improvising and composing;

   k be motivated to investigate other forms of music-making and listening.

The Teacher

1 *Growing with Music: Key Stage 1* provides the teacher with:

   a a repertoire of songs;

   b a course programme of skills and concepts;

   c practical teaching suggestions and other material.

2 The teacher will be selecting:

   a the songs to be learnt;

   b the skills and concepts to be taught;

   c an appropriate means for teaching and learning.

3 The teacher will be continuously assessing:

   a class progress;

   b individual child development.

4 It is hoped that *Growing with Music: Key Stage 1* will provide a core from which the teachers will be encouraged to explore ideas of their own and materials from other sources.

5 Although *Growing with Music: Key Stage 1* cannot in itself develop the *personal* vocal and musical skills of the teacher it can, through teacher appraisal and practice of its contents, develop the *professional* awareness of the place and purpose of music in education.

However, to teach with greater confidence, it is important that the teacher develops personal music skills and a knowledge of music. Teachers might find it helpful, therefore, to seek the advice and assistance of colleagues, and to approach local Advisory Teachers who will be able to advise regarding in-service support.

Key Stage 1 materials

The *Growing with Music* teaching materials for use at Key Stage 1 consist of the following items:

1 TEACHER'S BOOK
This includes:
Skill/Concept index
The Course } Course Programme
Song collection

Copymasters. This section includes:
Record of Content
Records of Assessment
Rhythm Cards
Reading Sheets

2 SONG COLLECTION ON CASSETTE

Skill/Concept index

This is a list of skills or concepts, identified as being essential to basic musical progress. It is in a sequential order, which makes the acquisition of skills and concepts easier for the child, and consequently builds a steady growth in confidence. The teacher will usually find it helpful, therefore, to adhere to the sequential order of the index, and should move to a new skill or concept according to the promptings of experience and instinct.

> ▷ At any given time, one is usually in the process of developing several skills and concepts. Generally speaking, the content of a lesson will reflect several stages of learning. The time required for the conscious acquisition of a skill or concept will vary. For example, Skill/Concept number 3 may take many months to develop; Skill/Concept number 5 may be established within several lessons.

The Course

This section presents the individual components of the *Skill/Concept index* with *Suggested songs/rhymes* and *Teaching ideas*.

Suggested songs/rhymes

These are recommended as providing the important base of experience from which the children's aural understanding and knowledge will largely grow. It is not necessary for the children to be familiar with all the items; nor does the list necessarily include all the possibilities in the song collection suitable for that Skill/Concept. It is essential that the songs/rhymes selected by the teacher for a Skill/Concept should be well assimilated by the children some time *before* any conscious teaching points are made.

Teaching ideas

These are arranged under two headings: KEY and FURTHER.

KEY Teaching ideas are commended to teachers as being those which have proved successful with children.

FURTHER Teaching ideas provide an enrichment of *KEY Teaching ideas* and will be useful when further practice is thought necessary.

When applied to a teaching situation:

1 The teaching ideas are not too detailed since it is assumed that:
  a each teaching situation is unique;
  b the generally understood skills of teaching apply in most cases;
  c a teacher should not be encumbered by too many instructions;
  d the teacher must be encouraged to make his/her own decisions.

2 The *Teaching ideas* give guidance on developing a skill or concept.

3 In many instances these ideas can and should be extended by the teacher.

4 The teacher should decide which of these ideas will best assist in developing a chosen skill or concept.

5 It is hoped that the teacher will introduce his/her own teaching ideas as experience grows.

Song collection

The songs and rhymes are for the children to make their own; indeed, many examples are derived directly, or in an adapted form, from the oral and aural traditions of children's culture – singing games, action songs and humorous songs. Some are songs with composed melodies and words, and these have been included in the collection for their verbal and melodic suitability to children of this age-range.

The first section of the *Song collection* contains recommended rhymes and songs which the teacher will find valuable for the conscious acquisition of the skills and concepts outlined in the *Course programme*.

The second section of the *Song collection* provides additional repertoire of equal validity to that of the first section, but offers a wider range of experience and a basis for future work in **Growing with Music: Key Stage 2A.**

The teacher who is prepared to sing and to share suitable songs with his/her children, and thus to extend the children's repertoire by personal vocal contact, will make a deep musical impression. For the teacher whose level of personal aural and reading skill does not yet extend to staff notation (as in the *Song collection*), a transcription of these songs is printed in rhythm-solfa notation immediately following the main song section.

Above all, the *Song collection* is a resource intended to provide a rich musical experience and much enjoyment.

Look for opportunities to add to the song repertoire in this programme, remembering that the choice is not confined by items in the *Skill/Concept index*. (We are reminded of the teacher who, mistakenly, said 'We may not sing that song – we have not done "compound time" yet!') However, care should be taken to choose songs which are good examples of their kind, which are of suitable pitch range, avoiding difficult intervals, and which have words appropriate to this age-range.

Do not forget to include songs from local culture.

The Song collection on cassette

All the songs in this Teacher's Book collection have been recorded on cassette, with the intention of making them more accessible to teachers – particularly to those who might have some initial difficulty in reading the melodies from staff notation. It is essential that the teacher knows the song material well and, since songs are best learnt by aural encounter, the cassette should prove helpful.

However, the children need to learn the songs directly from the teacher, so it is not recommended that the cassette is played to the children. There can be no substitute for the teacher's active involvement in the personal presentation of song repertoire to the class.

Copymasters

The copymasters at the end of this book may be photocopied by the teacher when needed. It is recommended that photocopies of the Rhythm Cards, for example, be mounted on card for better handling in class. Some copymasters are intended for child use and may be coloured by the child and kept in a file.

Reading sheets

For most of this course, it is not intended that the child should be concerned with the reading or writing of notation; at Key Stage 1 it is most important for the teacher to provide music experience through singing, movement, games and instrumental playing. However, when the child has a sufficiently wide base of aural experience, the visual image can play a unique part in reinforcing or establishing aural concepts, and in introducing basic notation. A number of copymasters are available for this purpose, as part of the teacher's course material. These are labelled 'Reading Sheet'. References are made occasionally in the *Course programme* to particular Reading Sheets, and the teacher's attention is drawn to the following code symbols which indicate the best way in which each Reading Sheet might be used:

1 Reading with the teacher.
These Reading Sheets are for the teacher to hold when working with a group of children or with the whole class. They could be enlarged to A3 size if necessary, and their appearance could be enhanced by adding colour.

2 Reading from sheets.
These Reading Sheets are for distribution to individual children, so that they read from their own sheet rather than from a common source – e.g. the board or overhead projector. Simple line drawings have been used so that the child might make the sheets more attractive by using colour or adding more detail. These could be used for display in the classroom, or for taking home.

Record of content

The Record of Content Charts (see *Copymasters*) make it possible for the teacher to record details of music curriculum content over a period of time. This can be helpful when reviewing work done or planning future sessions. These charts also serve as a useful record if, for example, the class changes teacher.

However, the Content Charts do not provide for the documentation of child progress. For this, please see *Assessment in the National Curriculum.*

Preparations for teaching

The learning process

Teachers should consider the four stages needed in the child's learning of a new concept.

A Preparing

Participating in games and activities as a context within which associated songs and rhymes are learned and assimilated.

B Making conscious

Developing a musical skill/concept, as a conscious process:
a by heightening the child's aural awareness and facility for inner hearing (with the use of appropriate physical activity);
b by use of visual symbols (sound with notation);
c by use of the appropriate musical term (sound/symbol with name).

C Reinforcing

Practising and developing the child's experience of a concept by repeating activities or making connections from associated activities.

D Using in a new situation

Practising and developing the child's experience of a skill/concept by:
a learning new songs;
b participating in new activities;
c improvising;
— and, when appropriate:
d reading;
e writing.

▷ The teaching procedure should follow a pattern over a period of time in which several concepts are being taught, so that at a given moment each concept has reached a different learning stage:

A	B	C	D			
	A	B	C	D		
		A	B	C	D	
			A	B	C	D

A = Preparing
B = Making conscious   D = Using in a new
C = Reinforcing   situation

Consequently, account will need to be taken of the child's process of learning when the teaching is prepared. The *Skill/Concept index* and the *Record of Assessment* will help, but the teacher should also consider the following:

1 The *Growing with Music: Key Stage 1* course is essentially aural in nature; in other words, music experiences are the priority – i.e. involvement in music activity appropriate to the age of the child. Reading and writing activity is suitable, but only towards the end of this phase – at a time when much music experience has been assimilated.

2 The child does not simply 'acquire' music on his/her own; it is necessary that the child is placed purposefully into a music learning situation. The role of the teacher is twofold: firstly, to provide the enrichment and the opportunity for music to take place (e.g. as with maths work), and secondly, to prepare a curriculum with a repertoire and a structure which promote learning, and which include modes of teaching appropriate to the age of the child.

3 By performing music for others, and by listening to the music of others, a sharing process takes place which is essential to personal musical progress and development.

The teaching session

1 Group the children together for optimum eye and voice contact.

2 Seat the children on chairs, where possible. This will aid breathing, vocal support and comfort. The children need to be aware from an early stage that posture is important for producing a good singing sound.

3 For activities requiring movement, such as singing games, use only the amount of space necessary to retain group focus.

4 When appropriate, begin the session with a familiar greeting and song.

5 Try to end the session at a point of obvious achievement.

Including music in topic work

Teachers using this music programme will quickly become aware of opportunities for including or integrating song material or music teaching ideas within topic work, whether it be class-based or school-based. For example, a topic about people could include songs such as 'Little Arabella Miller' and 'Willum he had seven sons'; a topic on animals could include many references to known songs.

Also, opportunities will present themselves from time to time for integrated activity with another aspect of the curriculum. For example, dance-movement techniques using heavy and slow or light and quick movements can be explored within a context of tempo, dynamics and rhythm.

In this way, the children will come to relate their music to other areas of experience and will be developing their musicianship within a context which is integrated rather than isolated.

Planning the lesson

There is no substitute for good preparation.

1 A planned 10–15 minutes session each day, preferably in the morning, is suggested. Nevertheless, opportunities for spontaneous singing should be taken as they arise. Never allow planning to stifle spontaneity.

2 'Little and often' is desirable for a learning process that makes great demands on the listening and aural thinking of teacher and child.

3 Good planning and teaching never makes learning difficult for children, but only fair and demanding. Plan ahead, so that you cater for the continuity of learning, but be flexible in your expectations of the children's abilities.

4 Have regard for the process of learning (see above), remembering:
   a the children's previous experience;
   b at any one time, different learning stages will have been reached – to varying levels of achievement;
   c the principles and intentions of *Growing with Music: Key Stage 1*;
   d the invaluable help that comes from seeking the advice and assistance of colleagues.

5 The Teacher Planning Chart (see *Copymasters*) provides the teacher with a way of setting out the information s/he needs to plan an effective music session. This should help achieve cohesion and direction in the teaching. An example of a completed planning chart is shown below.

Teacher planning chart	Class: *Year Two* Date: *10 March*		Objective: *To develop skills at improvising with pitch and to introduce the note 'lah'*	
Skill/Concept reference	**Preparing**	**Making conscious**	**Reinforcing**	**Using in a new situation**
Nos 1 and 2 *To stimulate a sense of pitch* *No 15* *To relate sounds of higher and lower pitch* *No 16* *To improvise with notes of known pitch* *No 18* *To introduce a new note*	*A* *Sing song 86 'Sally go round the sun'* *I* *Sing 'Alice the Camel' (song 96)*	*D* *15(c) 15(d) Using rhyme 7 'One potato'* *G* *18(a) Sing song 25 'Tick-tock, see my clock'* *H, Sing first phrase and rationalise 'lah'*	*B* *Improvising hummed phrases for children to 'catch' and repeat* *C, Song 43 'Hickety tickety'* *F* *Individuals to handsign phrases for class/individuals to sing back (sotfa)*	*E* *Child hums single sound and indicates to another to hum a second sound higher/lower/same*

Developing a musical ear

It is sometimes said of those who show a certain facility for music that they have 'a musical ear' – usually as an expression of admiration of musical ability or achievement.

However, the term also carries with it the implication that although most other people are normal (i.e. not lacking in anything), those with 'a musical ear' happen to be endowed with extra musical benefits. This is a common opinion which fuels the equally common, but mistaken, belief that musical giftedness is a prerequisite for making music. Obviously, musical giftedness exists. But the relativities of terms such as 'gifted', 'talented', 'musical', 'has a good ear' are generally used so loosely as to be meaningless.

It seems to be a reasonable assumption (borne out in our experience and observation) that, with few exceptions, all children start life with a great potential for musical growth and understanding. But, in a world in which the prevailing view is that only the few have a 'gift' for music, it is hardly surprising that it is only the few who find the opportunity to develop their natural potential.

Education, with its structure and institutions, exists to ensure that each new generation has the opportunity to grow – not only by haphazard coincidence (which has its value), but also by programmes of planned experience and discovery.

This course is such a programme, based on the belief that the teacher in school is well-placed to make a significant contribution to realising the great musical potential in all children. It identifies certain musical objectives which are basic to musical understanding and progress, discoverable and achievable by teacher and child, and fundamental and common to all musical styles.

The structure of the programme is evolved largely from the repertoire, and the *Teaching ideas* are prepared with children aged 4–7 in mind. Most activities are shared by the whole class, with the objective that each child will develop his/her personal musical potential; and a process of musical development is initiated which contains the seeds of substantial musical growth for later years (See **Growing with Music: Key Stage 2A/2B**).

When all have musical ears, music becomes accessible to all.

Course programme

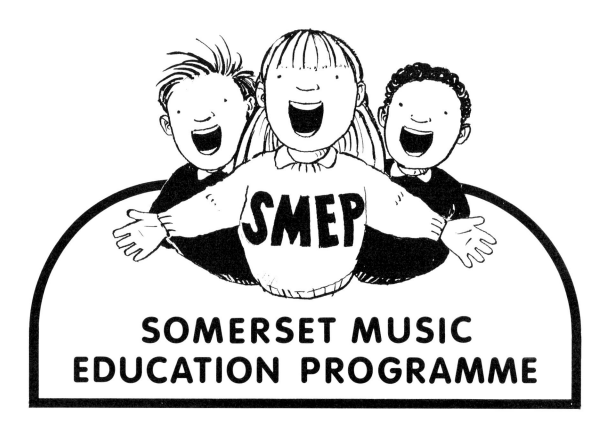

SOMERSET MUSIC
EDUCATION PROGRAMME

- The aim of the *Course programme* is to provide for the teacher a skeletal structure upon which the flesh of living musical experience can be assembled. The content of the *Course programme* needs to be placed within an imaginative context, for it is in this way that the teaching takes on the vitality necessary for younger children successfully to acquire musical skills and concepts. So, although the teacher is aware of the chain of musical events that s/he wishes to pursue, his/her preparation should ensure a presentation which is dramatic, descriptive and imaginative.

- Hence, games and imaginary situations are a means for experiencing, discovering and learning. A theme such as 'A Journey' or 'Sharing' can provide an imaginative link for a sequence of musical events concerned with, for example, developing an awareness of phrase length. The teaching should always strive to be imaginative and musical. 'Props' such as puppets, toys, pictures and balls will be invaluable.

Objective summary of *Growing with Music: Key Stage 1*

Voice	To find the singing voice. To develop the confidence to sing with accuracy and quality.
Ear	To develop an accurate and discriminatory aural sense.
Songs	To assimilate a large collection of songs and associated activities.
Phrase	To develop a feeling for and an awareness of phrase in melody and rhythm.
Pulse	To feel the pulse externally and internally. To discover the fundamental role of pulse in rhythm and melody.
Rhythm	To develop an awareness of rhythmic movement. To use the rhythm elements ♩ ♫ z (simple time), and ♩. ♫♪ z. (compound time) with their rhythm names. To perform rhythm exercises aurally and to improvise rhythm phrases.
Pitch	To develop the awareness of melodic shape and the aural concept of high and low. By means of aural development and the use of solfa, to understand the pitch relationships of **soh/me/lah.**
Literacy	To develop the reading and writing of rhythm phrases, using ♩ ♫ z / ♩. ♫♪ z. To read the 2-beat time-signature with bar lines (simple time only). To read and write melodic phrases using **soh/me/lah** in rhythm solfa.

Skill/Concept index – Key Stage 1

- The *Skill/Concept index* should be used in the knowledge that it is based on logical and musical principles, but that the order should not be adhered to rigidly if practical teaching sense suggests some deviation.

- Teachers should also be aware of the need to review established skills and concepts regularly, so as to exercise the memory, deepen understanding and extend ability still further.

- Although, at a given moment in time, the teaching plan is likely to be preoccupied with particular skills and concepts, overall, the outcome for the child should be one of musical achievements – the result of a continuing encounter with fundamentals such as phrase, pulse, rhythm, pitch, dynamics, timbre, and an accumulation of experience, skills and knowledge.

1 **Finding the voice: class/group vocal pitch-matching.**

2 **Finding the voice: individual vocal pitch-matching.**

3 **Developing an awareness of phrase length. Cultivating a controlled, unbroken singing sound, using one breath per melodic phrase.**

4 **Feeling, recognising and performing a steady pulse.**

5 **Distinguishing louder and quieter.**

6 **Distinguishing faster and slower (tempo). Feeling the pulse internally and making conscious the pulse.**

7 **Pitch: an awareness of melodic shape – moving down/moving up/moving on the same note.**

8 **Distinguishing pulse and rhythm.**

9 **Feeling the *rest* as an aural feature of phrase.**

10 **Simple time: identifying the pattern of two notes to one pluse (aural).**

11 **Simple time: identifying rhythms by their names (*ta ti-ti*).**

12 **Simple time: introducing the quarter-note (crotchet) and eighth-note (quaver) rhythm symbols to represent the rhythm names (*ta-ti-ti*).**

13 **Simple time: sense of metre – feeling the strong beat.**
Introducing the bar line in simple time $\frac{2}{4}$.

14 **Simple time: the quarter-note (crotchet) rest as a symbol and its place in written phrases (z).**

15 **Pitch: distinguishing higher and lower by large gesture and symbol.**

16 **Pitch: identifying the minor third by pitch names (*soh* and *me*) supported by their handsigns.**

17 **Compound time: feeling and recognising compound time patterns (aural).**

18 **Pitch: introduction of *lah* with handsign: *l–s–m* (aural).**

19 **Compound time: the pattern of three notes to one pulse, using rhythm names (*ti-ti-ti/tai*); introducing rhythm notation (⊓⊓ l.) and the rest (z.).**

20 **Phrase: feeling, recognising and counting phrases.**

21 **Melody: constructing melodic phrases by combining pitch and rhythm elements, and writing them by combining pitch and rhythm symbols (rhythm-solfa) – simple time only.**

The Course

Skill/Concept

1   Finding the voice: class/group vocal pitch-matching.

2   Finding the voice: individual vocal pitch-matching.

Suggested songs/rhymes

1	Hello, how are you?
2	Cobbler, cobbler
7	One potato
16	Round and round
28	Here we go
34	Who is that I see?
35	Engine, engine
37	Who has the penny?
38	Here is the beehive
43	Hickety tickety
53	Glowing candle-light
65	Hey! Hey! Look at me!
67	Here I come
70	Rat-a-tat-tat!
75	Sleep, baby, sleep

Teaching ideas

KEY ▶

1 a   Sing a song at three different pitches (that is, using a new starting note for three successive performances).

1 b   Select groups of children to sing imitatively a melodic phrase of a song.

2 a   Select one child to sing imitatively a melodic phrase of a song. For most children a phrase from an established song is often more appropriate than a song which is in the early stages of being learnt.

FURTHER ▶

2 b   Invite individuals to sing a song of their choice from the *Song collection*.

> ▷ **A Song Collage:** As the children begin to acquire a repertoire of songs, a composite collage may be made of pictures representing the subject matter of chosen songs – using for examples children's drawings and magazine cut-outs.

2 c   Using response songs (question-and-answer songs, such as 'Hickety tickety'), encourage vocal pitch-matching between individuals and between an individual and the class. This is particularly useful when a child is at an early stage of finding the singing voice and attempts to pitch-match another child who has a secure sense of vocal pitch.

1 / 2 a   Improvising. Play 'Who has the penny?' from the *Song collection*.

1 / 2 b   Improvising. Encourage individuals to improvise a melody for the words of a greeting, which is then appropriately answered by the class using the same melody.

1 / 2 c   Encourage individual children to pick a song title from a 'lucky dip'. The child sings the song and this is repeated by the class or another child. The 'lucky dip' contains titles of well-known songs on slips of papers; other titles can be added as more songs are assimilated.

1 / 2 c   Sing a rhyme on one note only as an exercise in pitch-matching. When secure, repeat the rhyme at a different pitch level.

> ▷ The individual efforts of children, whether imitating or improvising, should always engage the appreciation of the other children.
>
> This will happen when:
> **a** there are frequent opportunities to perform as an individual;
> **b** the opportunities to perform as individuals are made available to everyone over a period of time (normally avoiding the temptation to ask for volunteers);
> **c** individual performances are a regular and expected occurrence;
> **d** the children are encouraged to listen and to comment with the involvement of the individual performer in an objective and appreciative way;
> **e** the children are involved in making agreed corrections in a way which is musically aware and sensitive.

Skill/Concept

3   Developing an awareness of phrase length.
Cultivating a controlled, unbroken singing sound, using one breath
per melodic phrase.

Suggested songs/rhymes

8   To market
20   Rain on the green grass
23   Jack-in-the-box
28   Here we go
33   Lots of rosy apples
35   Engine, engine
51   Once a man fell in a well
92   One little candle

(For this concept all songs are suitable)

▷ With some songs and rhymes the phrase length
is a matter of interpretation.

Teaching ideas

KEY ▶

3 **a**   Arrange for two groups to sing alternate phrases of a song.

3 **b**   Movement. The flow and duration of phrases is best expressed in movement by torso and arm movements. Find smooth, sustained movements with which the children are familiar (e.g. pushing, pulling, drawing in sand, painting with long strokes). During the activity it is important to retain the children's eye contact.

3 **c**   Movement. Sing the first phrase of a song while walking a circle in one direction; sing the next phrase while walking in the opposite direction, and so on. For a clear and orderly start to each new phrase it will be necessary to have a very short pause. Encourage a breath to be taken only at the change of phrase.

3 **d**   Movement. The phrase 'sets out' and 'arrives'. The children sit in a circle or group. One child leaves his/her place and performs a locomotor movement in a certain shape or direction, timing the return to coincide with the end of the phrase.

3 **e**   Arrange for two individuals to sing alternate phrases of a song.

3 **f**   Movement. Devise other movements or actions to help children visualise the duration of the phrase as it is performed. For example, geometric shapes or numbers can be traced in the air or on the floor – a circle for younger children; a figure 6 for older children.

3 g   Ask a child to draw on the board a rainbow shape for each melodic phrase of a song, as it is sung by the class, e.g. ⌒ . In a similar way, the class may trace this shape through the air as they sing. Encourage children to breathe only before the start of each 'rainbow', i.e. phrase.

3 h   In addition to working with melodic phrases, the children should work with rhythm phrases, normally performed by tapping and without using words. These can be taken from songs and rhymes in the *Song collection* using the ideas suggested above.

FURTHER ▶

3 i   Instruments. Use non-pitched percussion instruments to play the rhythm phrase of a song/rhyme. An instrument of different timbre is selected for each new phrase.

3 j   Listening. A piece is required in which the lengths of melodic phrases can be heard clearly. This is more likely to be obvious in solo melody, vocal or instrumental, and should be expressively performed.

> ▷ Encourage singing with a quiet and controlled voice. This enables children to achieve a greater degree of aural perception and consequent pitching accuracy. The singing of melodic phrases to a single vowel (such as 'noo'), or by humming, is useful in this respect.
>
> Please refer to *The singing sound* page 157.

Skill/Concept

4 Feeling, recognising and performing a steady pulse.

Suggested songs/rhymes

6 Twiddle-di-dee
10 See-saw
24 Can you tap your fingers?
26 This is how a drummer-boy/girl
42 Chuffa, chuffa, chuff!
63 An elephant goes like this
66 Teddy Bear, Teddy Bear
78 Hammering here
83 See the Indian chief

▷ Some children experience difficulty in keeping to a steady pulse. This could reflect muscular tension, but probably originates from a lack of aural focus. A percussion instrument, played by the teacher or by a child, will highlight the movement of the pulse in a distinctive way.

Teaching ideas

KEY ▶

4 a Movement. Perform a song or rhyme. Encourage the children to mark the pulse using a variety of large and small movements (e.g. rocking arms gently from side to side; tapping various parts of the body). Clapping is not recommended.

4 b Perform a song with one group tapping the pulse only and a second group singing only.

4 c Movement. With an agreed song in mind an individual child performs locomotor movements to a steady pulse, thus establishing a tempo. While observing this, the class performs the agreed song in the tempo which has been set.

FURTHER ▶

4 d Movement. In action songs and singing games, make movements with the pulse, as appropriate.

4 e Perform a song or rhyme with tapped pulse and eyes closed throughout.

4 f Movement. To a well-known action song such as 'I wiggle my shoulders' and using the thinking voice only (see page 155), perform actions with the pulse.

4 g Movement improvising. When the children are confident invite them to perform locomotor and other large movements to the pulse of known songs.

Skill/Concept

| 5 | Distinguishing louder and quieter. |

Suggested songs/rhymes

8   To market
21 I see you
23 Jack-in-the-box
41 A goblin lives in our house
52 Hush, my dear
53 Glowing candle-light
64 I wiggle my fingers
72 Little pony, gallop home
94 Farmer Higgs

▷ **Dynamics:** Distinguishing louder and quieter sounds presents no conceptual difficulty for children. Great contrast of volume is not recommended for children's voices as this tends to encourage shouting and breathy singing tone. Similarly, extremes of dynamic contrast can exceed the natural limitations of instruments, and are therefore musically undesirable. However, within limits, louder and quieter sounds can help in the understanding of musical structure (for example, to identify phrase lengths in a song), and both teacher and children should always be aware of the contribution that considered dynamic levels can make to the expressive quality of music.

Teaching ideas

KEY ▶

| 5 | a | Instruments. Compare louder and quieter sounds using percussion instruments. |

| 5 | b | Explore the contrasts between the whispering, shouting, speaking, singing and humming voices. Also, discover the dynamic contrasts within each one of these voices. |

| 5 | c | Movement. Loud or quiet sounds using instruments can be represented in movements which are strong or gentle, tense or relaxed and heavy or light. Perform the same movement in these contrasting ways. |

FURTHER ▶

| 5 | d | Quietly sing the first melodic phrase of a known song, singing the next phrase more loudly; alternate in this way with further phrases. |

| 5 | e | Play the game of opposites: e.g. sing a phrase loudly; the group imitates quietly (and vice versa). |

$\boxed{5}$ **f**　Movement. Find contrasting strong and gentle movements to accompany different verses of a song sung at different dynamic levels.

> ▷ Older children will find a wide contrast of singing volume easier to achieve without resorting to a shout. Teachers may feel *Teaching ideas* $\boxed{5}$ **d, e** and **f** are inappropriate for younger children in this age-range.

$\boxed{5}$ **g**　**Crescendo** – gradually becoming louder.

Diminuendo – gradually becoming quieter.

Both can be explored using any of the above ideas.

$\boxed{5}$ **h**　Movement. **Accent** – a sudden louder sound. Ask the children to crouch down and sing quietly. On the last note of the song they jump up to a loud percussion sound.

$\boxed{5}$ **i**　Movement. Find those words in a song which can be distinctively louder or quieter. Mark the word with an appropriate movement and accompany with a percussion instrument sound.

$\boxed{5}$ **j**　Movement. Devise movement games which involve a quick response to a sudden, loud signal. Similar games may be played with a quiet signal.

Skill/Concept

6 Distinguishing faster and slower (tempo).
Feeling the pulse internally and making conscious the pulse.

Suggested songs/rhymes

5   Chop, chop, choppety chop!
14 Snail, snail
24 Can you tap your fingers?
25 Tick-tock, tick-tock, see my clock
27 Rabbit in the hollow
42 Chuffa, chuffa, chuff!
52 Hush, my dear
70 Rat-a-tat-tat!
85 Sally go round the sun
87 Oats and beans

▷ **Tempo** is the pulse speed. Children should experience faster and slower tempi at all stages of development. The character of a song will influence the tempo used. An inappropriate tempo can be disastrous for the song, and for its musical and subject content. Individuals should be invited to set the tempo of known songs and the children asked to consider the most appropriate tempo.

Teaching ideas

▷ Young children have difficulty synchronising larger movements in a tempo very much faster or slower than their own natural tempo.

KEY ▶

6 a Movement. Invite children to find their own slow or quick walking speeds, without a predetermined tempo. Use dramatic ideas to encourage slow steps.

6 b Perform a song several times to a slow pulse and then to a quick(er) pulse. Individual children might be invited to set the tempo; for example, ask a child to tap or walk an agreed number of pulses before a song begins.

6 c To encourage the internal feeling for a steady tempo, the class (group or individual child) listens carefully as the teacher (individual child) sings the first phrase of a known song – then the class sings the next phrase without hesitation or variation of pace.

6 **d** Perform a song to an agreed silent pulse movement (e.g. swaying).

FURTHER ▶ **6** **e** Movement. The teacher plays or sings for the children and varies the tempo, making sudden changes. The children respond to each tempo, using movements on the spot (e.g. sawing wood, chopping). A similar game might be played using gradual changes in tempo (**accelerando/rallentando**).

6 **f** Show four heart-shape symbols on the board (each representing a pulse) thus:

Reading from left to right, invite a child to touch the symbols in tempo, while the class sings a song chosen for its 4-beat phrases.

Skill/Concept

| 7 | Pitch: an awareness of melodic shape – moving down/moving up/ moving on the same note.

Suggested songs/rhymes

22 Bells in the steeple
23 Jack-in-the-box
28 Here we go
31 Little Arabella Miller
39 Bow, wow, wow!
45 Ding, dong
51 Once a man fell in a well
54 Pancake Tuesday
55 Willum he had seven sons
92 One little candle

Teaching ideas

KEY ▶

7 **a** Demonstrate a low humming voice sliding upwards in pitch to a high voice and vice versa. Ask the children to copy.

7 **b** With the children, speak the rhyme 'One potato'. Improvise a melody of descending shape for the first phrase and ask the children to imitate. Now sing an ascending melody for the second phrase, and ask the children to imitate. Ask the children about what they heard and felt the voice doing: establish the language of 'moving down' and 'moving up'. Repeat the above, but using a down and up movement of the hand to illustrate visually the movement of the melody. Finally, sing a phrase on one note. Let the children do the same and ask for their reactions: establish the language of 'moving on the same note'.

7 **c** Movement. Ask the children to respond in movement to a **glissando** (up *and* down) on a xylophone, swannee whistle or keyboard.

7 **d** Movement. Sing known song phrases which incorporate moving down, moving up and moving on the same note – using movement activity, finger-painting in the air, drawing on the board, and the 'chime-bar staircase' (see next page) to support the listening.

FURTHER ▶

7 **e** Movement. Using a piano, voice or other instrument, the teacher improvises a melodic phrase which is then repeated while the children improvise appropriate movement activities.

7 **f** Instruments. With the children's help, build a 'chime-bar staircase' using, for example, books or wood. The chime-bar with the lowest sounding pitch should be placed at the bottom, and the others rising by step and pitch to the highest. Thus, chime-bars with the note names C D E F G are arranged to appear to the children in this way:

29

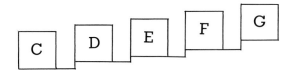

Demonstrate ascending and descending phrases from known songs on the 'chime-bar staircase' (e.g. 'Once a man fell in a well'), but ask the children to sing the phrase first.

7 g Instruments. While the rest of the children have closed eyes, invite a child to play the 'chime-bar staircase' from low to high/high to low by step. When the phrase is played again the children hum it, moving their hands up and down accordingly. Finally, they check their thinking with eyes open as the phrase is played once more. This game should be played using other pitched instruments also, e.g. xylophone, piano.

7 h Help the children to experiment with well-known sounds of changing pitch, imitating with their voices and/or instruments, e.g. the sound of a motor-car or other machines.

> ▷ **Instruments:** When appropriate, involve children in selecting the instruments they feel are most suitable for the task, and to give their reasons. This will presume that previous experiences have made them familiar with the sounds and technique of playing each of the instruments available to them. For guidance in the use of instruments refer to page 163.

Skill/Concept

8   Distinguishing pulse and rhythm.

Suggested songs/rhymes

5   Chop, chop, choppety chop!
6   Twiddle-di-dee
9   I, I, me oh my!
30   Listen, listen, here I come
31   Little Arabella Miller
68   Here I come

▷ Please remember that the performing of rhythm should always be to an established tempo.

Teaching ideas

▷ It is important that children frequently experience through tapping and movement the rhythm of phrases from songs and rhymes.

KEY ▶

8 **a**   Selecting a phrase from a known song or rhyme, the children *speak* the words rhythmically to a steady pulse. They repeat this and simultaneously tap the rhythm. In a similar way perform other examples.

8 **b**   Sing a melodic phrase; tap its rhythm; sing the phrase again.

8 **c**   Improvising. Improvise a 4-beat tapped rhythm-phrase (using ♩ ♫) for the children to repeat. Further phrases might be similarly improvised and performed using a variety of body-sounds. Do not forget to work with individuals as well as with the whole class.

▷ Please see *Glossary* (page 165) on the use of the words **beat** and **pulse** as used in this course.

8 **d**   Using the first part of a song or rhyme, one group taps the pulse while a second group taps the rhythm (using a different sound). Without pause, the roles are reversed for the second part of the song.

8 **e**   Movement. Perform a chosen song with actions intended to help distinguish pulse and rhythm, changing the action for each new performance (or verse).

The following actions are suggested:

    (i) sing the song, stepping the pulse;

    (ii) sing the song, tapping the rhythm (two fingers on palm of hand);

    (iii) sing the song, tapping the pulse (on the shoulder);

    (iv) step the pulse, tapping the rhythm (two fingers on palm of hand);

and for older or more experienced children –

    (v) step the pulse, singing the song (silently with the thinking voice).

FURTHER ▶

8 f A child sings a known song while a second child identifies and taps the pulse. Then, with the first child singing the same song, a second child identifies and taps the rhythm.

8 g Choose three songs with different and distinctive rhythms. Ask the class to sing the three songs. Then, perform the rhythm only of one of the songs, inviting the children to use their thinking voices to identify the melody, and when they feel sure they have identified it, to join in by singing the melody. Invite an individual to lead a similar activity with one of the other songs.

8 h The children are asked to identify a known song performed by the teacher using:

   (i) thinking voice only;

  (ii) tapped pulse only;

 (iii) tapped rhythm only;

 (iv) sung melody.

What do the children notice?
(Answer: It is only possible to identify the song from hearing **(iii)** and **(iv)**.)

8 i Instruments. Invite a child to play the rhythm of a song on a percussion instrument. A second child is then asked to identify and perform the pulse of the song simultaneously with the first child, upon an instrument of contrasting timbre. The distinction can be drawn many times using other instruments.

Children may be helped with the distinction by using:

Pulse	Rhythm
Tapped knees (Tambour)	Tapped palm (Claves)

Skill/Concept

9 Feeling the rest as an aural feature of phrase.

Suggested songs/rhymes

32 I have a dog
34 Who is that I see?
38 Here is the beehive
39 Bow, wow, wow!
47 Pease pudding hot
53 Glowing candle-light
66 Teddy Bear, Teddy Bear
70 Rat-a-tat-tat!

Teaching ideas

KEY ▶

9 a While singing a song, make a distinctive gesture (e.g. touching the shoulders) with a deliberate but quiet inhalation of breath for each rest.

9 b Instruments. Ask a child with an instrument to make one sound for each rest as it occurs during the singing of a song.

9 c Movement. Ask the class to form a circle with unjoined hands. While the class sings a known song, a child weaves in and out of the circle, and on the occasion of each rest taps the shoulder of the nearest child, who joins on as in 'Follow my leader'.

> ▷ Please remember that the rest is a feature of rhythm; the pulse continues throughout. Gestures and sounds are used only to highlight the concept of 'rest' and should be used discreetly, and only for as long as is necessary

9 d Instruments. Combine three suitable and distinctive-sounding instruments, one to play the rhythm of a song, another to play once for each rest, and a third to keep a steady pulse. On repeated performances, first eliminate the 'rest' instrument; on a subsequent repeat, eliminate both the 'rest' and 'pulse' instruments together – leaving the rhythm on its own.

FURTHER ▶

9 e The children, facing each other in pairs, with arms outstretched and hands poised above the opposite shoulders, sing a known song – tapping the shoulders of their partners when they are aware of a rest. The tempo should be slower in the early examples.

Skill/Concept

10   Simple time: identifying the pattern of two notes to one pulse (aural).

11   Simple time: identifying rhythms by their names (*ta ti-ti*).

Suggested songs/rhymes

10   See-saw
13   Rap-a tap-a
15   Rain, rain, go away!
26   This is how a drummer-boy/girl
31   Little Arabella Miller
44   See my wellingtons
49   Pitter, patter
50   Clip, clop
83   See the Indian chief

Teaching ideas

KEY ▶

10 a   Use 'playwords' in extracts of 4 beats' length from known songs and which involve ♩ ♫ only. For example:

Rhythm: | | ⌐⌐ |

Words: See   my   wel-ling-tons

Playwords: Clump, clump, clum-py, clump

   (i) sing the extract with words;
   (ii) sing the extract with playwords;
   (iii) speak the extract with playwords, drawing attention to the point at which two notes occur to the pulse ('clumpy').

(Also, see 'Rain, rain, go away!' Use 'drip, drop, drippy drop' for playwords.)

10 b   Draw on the board a visual representation of the 'playwords'. For example:

10 **c** Instruments. The children form two concentric circles, facing each other. One child in the centre maintains a steady pulse on a tambour. The members of one circle tap one sound to each pulse and the others tap a pattern of two sounds of equal length to each pulse. It is then useful for the children to hear this exercise played by three instruments of varying timbre.

☆ **Refer Reading Sheets 1 and 2**

> ▷ Please remember that rhythm work should always be done to an established and commonly felt tempo.

11 **a** With short extracts from known songs (using ♩ ♫ only):

(**i**) sing the extract using words; the class repeats;

(**ii**) sing the extract to 'noo'; the class repeats;

(**iii**) tap the rhythm phrase; the class repeats;

(**iv**) speak the phrase to rhythm names (**ta ti-ti**); the class repeats.

11 **b** Improvising. The teacher (and later a child) improvises rhythm-phrases of 4-beat length. The following sequence of ideas may be helpful:

Teacher/child	Class
Rhythm words	Rhythm words
Rhythm words	Tapping
Tapping	Tapping followed by rhythm words
Tapping	Rhythm words followed by tapping

FURTHER ▶

11 **c** The children perform a rhythm-phrase (using ♩ ♫ only) in imitation of the teacher. The phrase is then repeated at a different tempo. Ensure that if a slower tempo is chosen, the ♫ rhythm is even.

11 **d** Improvising.

(**i**) Initiate 'echo work' using 4-beat rhythm-phrases between a leader and the class, or between two children.

(**ii**) The children form a circle and a suitable drum is placed in the centre. A beater is passed round as the following is chanted:

The child receiving the beater at the end of the chant goes to the centre as the class sings 'This is how a drummer-boy/girl' (*Song collection* 26). Immediately following, and in the tempo of the song, the child improvises a 4-beat rhythm-phrase on the drum. The children repeat the phrase, first by tapping and then by speaking the rhythm names.

Skill/Concept

12 Simple time: introducing the quarter-note (crotchet) and eighth-note (quaver) rhythm symbols to represent the rhythm names (*ta ti-ti*).

> ▷ The names 'quarter note' and 'eighth note' (instead of 'crotchet' and 'quaver') are recommended. The teacher should refer to a written symbol by its musical term as soon as s/he feels the children can understand the information and use it. However, when performing rhythm-phrases continue to speak the rhythm language (**ta ti-ti**).

Teaching ideas

KEY ▶   **12** **a**   To introduce the written symbol:

Teacher	Class	on board
Taps ♩ ♩ ♩ ♩	Speaks rhythm names	
	Teacher writes symbols on board as class speaks	
	(i) class reads and speaks rhythm	| | | |
	(ii) class reads and taps rhythm	
Taps ♫♩ ♫♩ ♩ ♩ (or something similar)	Speaks rhythm names	
	Teacher writes symbols on board as class speaks	
	(i) class reads and speaks rhythm	⊓ ⊓ | |
	(ii) class reads and taps rhythm	
	Teacher repeats, using other examples.	

Examples for the teacher to use:		Child writes on board:
		♡ ♡ ♡ ♡
U1	♩ ♩ ♩ ♩	| | | |
U2	♩ ♩ ♫♩ ♩	| | ⊓ |
U3	♫♩ ♩ ♫♩ ♩	⊓ | ⊓ |
U4	♫♩ ♫♩ ♩ ♩	⊓ ⊓ | |

12 b The teacher selects 4-beat rhythm-phrases from known songs. The class:

> **(i)** sings the phrase using words;

> **(ii)** sings the phrase to 'noo';

> **(iii)** taps the rhythm-phrase as the teacher points to the beat visually represented on the board – see *Teaching idea* **6 f**;

> **(iv)** repeats the rhythm names of the phrase performed by the teacher, who simultaneously points to the beats on the board. A child is invited to write the rhythm on the board, using rhythm symbols;

> **(v)** speaks the written phrase using rhythm names.

☆ **Refer Reading Sheet 3**

12 c Lollipop sticks or short straws can be used by the children to construct:

> **(i)** 4-beat extracts from known songs containing | ⊓ rhythms only;

> **(ii)** 4-beat phrases performed or improvised by the teacher (and later by an individual child) using | ⊓ rhythms only – see **U1–U4**.

> ▷ The development of memory, i.e. an ability to retain rhythm or melodic phrases for a short period of time, is essential to the process of musical thinking.

12 d Improvising: Individual children improvise a tapped rhythm-phrase of 4-beat length as the teacher indicates the pulse. The class echoes with rhythm names and the rhythm is then notated by the child on the board. The phrase is labelled with the name of the composer (improviser). Alternatively, the class echoes and each child then notates the phrase on paper – or with sticks or short straws.

FURTHER ▶

12 e Invite a group of children to be 'rhythm-people' and construct phrases of 4-beat length from known songs, which the class reads with rhythm names; for example:

Speak: **ta   ti-ti   ti-ti   ta**

The children should perform the phrase to an established and *consistent* tempo. They will be helped in this (when necessary) if the teacher marks the pulse by gently tapping a tambour.

12 f Using rhythm cards:

> **(i)** the class reads from cards as they are shown;

> **(ii)** (memory training) the teacher shows a card, hides it, and the children speak or tap the rhythm after a short pause;

> **(iii)** the class is asked to identify known songs from performed rhythm extracts read from a rhythm card.

> ▷ There are many ways to use rhythm cards. Teachers are invited to use their imaginations in devising helpful games. Remember, reading should always be from left to right. Some cards may be inverted to produce new rhythms (simple time only).

Skill/Concept

13 Simple time: sense of metre – feeling the strong beat.

Introducing the bar line in simple time $\frac{2}{4}$.

Suggested songs/rhymes

Simple time: $\frac{2}{4}$

3   Jelly on a plate
36   Tom cats, alley cats
50   Clip, clop
55   Willum he had seven sons

Simple time: $\frac{3}{4}$

22   Bells in the steeple
45   Ding, dong
93   Oh, there are four seasons

Simple time: $\frac{4}{4}$

34   Who is that I see?
38   Here is the beehive
54   Pancake Tuesday

Teaching ideas

▷ Up to this stage, only 4-beat written phrases have been used, since reading longer phrases without bar lines can be confusing. The introduction of the bar line, therefore, will allow for longer phrases to be read.

▷ The position of the written bar lines should be arrived at by feeling strong and weak beats in melodic phrases and rhythm-phrases. This is much more musical than merely counting out the beats per bar, and establishes the concept of 'metre'.

KEY▶

13 a Movement. Sing a song, using appropriate movements to draw attention to the strong first beat within the metre. Many work-actions fall into this category.

13 b Movement. Devise tapping routines with a strong arm movement on the strong beat, followed by a weaker movement. For example, sitting on the floor:

(i) strike the floor on the first beat and tap the knees on the second to show a metre of 2;

(ii) similarly, 'strike, tap, tap' to show a metre of 3;

(iii) 'strike, tap, tap, tap' to show a metre of 4.

13 c Movement. Ask the children to translate their feeling for metre into a strong downward movement on the strong beat (using one hand, like a conductor's down-beat), while singing known songs.

13 d Using only songs in $\frac{2}{4}$ time and known rhythm symbols (♩ ♫), the teacher uses the down-beat movement to draw bar lines on the board while the children sing and conduct. The rhythm of the song is then written within the bar lines.

13 e Written rhythm phrases **U5–U10** are read from the board and the strong/weak beats felt (perhaps using body-sounds). The teacher draws bar lines so that the strong beat occurs at the beginning of each bar. A double bar line is inserted after the final beat.

The class can now see easily that there are two beats to each bar, and the figure 2 is accordingly written at the beginning of the phrase.

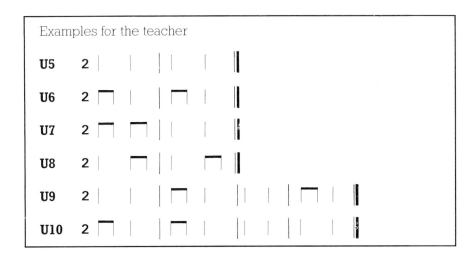

☆   **Refer Reading Sheets 4–7**

FURTHER ▶

13 f Movement. The teacher assembles a medley of known songs with successive changes of metre.

Each song is first sung separately with the children using an agreed form of movement activity to identify the metre. The children then perform the medley and show in movement (either directed or improvised) the successive changes of metre. It may be helpful to the children's memory if the first few words of each song are visually displayed.

13 g Instruments. Having sung a known song and (through movement) having decided on the metre, select three instruments of varying timbre. One is chosen to mark the pulse, another to reinforce the first beat of the metre, and the third to play the rhythm-phrases of the song. Three instrumentalists may then accompany as the others sing.

Skill/Concept

14 Simple time: the quarter-note (crotchet) rest as a symbol and its place in written phrases (*z*).

Suggested songs/rhymes

3 Jelly on a plate
4 Mice, mice
21 I see you
39 Bow, wow, wow!
42 Chuffa, chuffa, chuff!
47 Pease pudding hot
83 See the Indian chief

Teaching ideas

> ▷ Please note that the rest (simple time and compound time) is a feature of rhythm. In earlier stages it is helpful if the rest is voiced in an appropriate way; a recommendation is to use 'mm' as a quiet, almost inaudible sound.

KEY ▶

14 a With short extracted phrases from known songs (| ⊓ *z*) only:

  (i) sing the phrase using words;

  (ii) tap the phrase (with appropriate gesture for the rest);

  (iii) speak the phrase with rhythm names;

  (iv) the teacher writes the phrase on the board using rhythm symbols, drawing particular attention to the symbol for the rest.

  ☆ **Refer Reading Sheet 8**

14 b Using examples **U11–U15** tap 4-beat phrases for the children to repeat to rhythm names. One child writes the rhythm on the board. In a similar way further 4-beat examples may then be improvised by the teacher or individual children, and forms of notation constructed by using:

  (i) lollipop sticks;

  (ii) a team of 'rhythm people'

  e.g.

14 c   Improvising. Play 'Spot the Composer' game. Individual children improvise a tapped (or spoken) rhythm-phrase of 4-beat length as the teacher indicates the pulse. The class echoes with rhythm names and the rhythm is then notated by the improviser on the blackboard and by the children on paper. The class performs the written rhythm, thus verifying its accuracy. The phrase is then labelled with the name of the composer (improviser). Several phrases are thus entered on the board and on the children's paper. The teacher (or a child) then chooses and performs one of the phrases; the class identifies it by naming the composer.

☆   **Refer Reading Sheets 9 and 10**

FURTHER ▶

14 d   Using the *Teaching idea* **12** **f** the children read rhythm cards which include the z.

14 e   Write on the board a rhythm-phrase from a well-known song, but omitting a distinctive rhythm motif, for example:

2 | | | | z | | | ‖
Bow,   wow,   wow! . . . . .

or

Lit - tle Tom-my Tuck-er's dog . . . . .   wow!

The children sing the complete melodic phrase; they then speak the rhythm names of the phrase and an individual is invited to write in the missing motif.

14 f   Display several rhythm reading cards. The teacher or a child performs the rhythm of one of the cards; the class identifies the card chosen.

☆   **Refer Reading Sheets 11–13**

41

Skill/Concept

15   Pitch: distinguishing higher and lower by large gesture and symbol.

Suggested songs/rhymes

10   See-saw
11   Cuckoo! Cherry tree
19   Roll up! Here's the fair
20   Rain on the green grass

Teaching ideas

> ▷ Mistakenly, young children often use the words 'louder' and 'softer' or 'bigger' and 'smaller' to describe changes in pitch.

KEY ▶

15 a   Sing a higher sound with hand held high, and then a lower sound with the hand held low. Ask the children to show by the same gestures which sound they hear.

15 b   Ask a child to imitate the singing of a higher sound with hand held high, and then a lower sound with the hand held low.

15 c   Sing a short rhyme on one repeated note, e.g. 'One potato'. Repeat, but alter the pitch up or down for one of the words, and ask the children on which word the note was changed. Ask them to sing the example, and to say whether the sound of their voice went up or down. Sing once more, with hand gestures to illustrate the change of note.

15 d   Ask a child to sing one line of a rhyme on one note. Ask a second child to sing the next line of the rhyme at a different pitch. Ask the class if the second line was higher or lower in pitch.

FURTHER ▶

15 e   Use a high and a low note on the piano or xylophone to give two signals, e.g. 'high' for stand up; 'low' for sit down.

15 f   Sing improvised slow-moving melodies using two notes only, one of higher pitch and one of lower pitch. The hand is held high or low as the melody progresses.

15 g   Instruments. Ask a child to play two chime bars of different pitch and to decide how to place them on two surfaces of different height to show the higher and lower sounds. Ask the children to check the pitch of the sound as the bars are played again.

15 h Introduce the children to the written concepts of high and low pitch:

(i) Higher

Lower

On a board or large sheet of paper draw 'blobs' as illustrated.

(ii) The teacher hums two notes of the same pitch, and shows the first note on the left and the second note on the right, thus:

(iii) Now, two notes of different pitch can be similarly represented.

In this way, two visual concepts are taught – 'higher' and 'lower', and reading from left to right.

(iv) These ideas are repeated with the children imitating the teacher's humming and one child invited to draw the 'blobs' as appropriate.

> ▷ Wider intervals should be used at first (e.g. octave, sixth or fifth). With experience, gradually introduce smaller intervals until the minor third is arrived at (**s–m**).

Skill/Concept

16 Pitch: identifying the minor third by pitch names (*soh* and *me*) supported by their handsigns.

Suggested songs/rhymes

9 I, I, me oh my!

10 See-saw

11 Cuckoo! Cherry tree

12 Pears for pies

65 Hey! Hey! Look at me!

66 Teddy Bear, Teddy Bear

67 Here I come

Teaching ideas

Handsigns are of value in supporting and reinforcing the habit-memory for intervals. They are, however, rather inadequate for showing all but the simplest of rhythm features.

The position of the hand moves according to the degree of the scale being represented.

lah ——— Eye height

soh ——— Chin height

me ——— Chest height

The children should be encouraged at all times to sing and to think in melodic phrases. The handsigns should therefore move smoothly and expressively.

KEY ▶

16 **a** Sing a phrase/extract from a (s–m) song, with the following sequence:

  (i) class sings the song with words;

  (ii) teacher sings using pitch names (solfa);

(iii) class repeats;

(iv) repeat **(ii)** and **(iii)** with handsigns.

> ▷ **Solfa** is a singing language. When using pitch names during instructions or explanations, sing them rather than speak them, encouraging the children to do likewise.

Examples for the teacher

U16 s–m–s

U17 s–s–m–m

U18 s–m–s–s

U19 m–s–m

U20 m–m–s

16 b Using short improvised phrases (**s–m**): e.g. (**U16–U20**):

Teacher	Class/group/individual
(i) Sings a short phrase using pitch names.	**(i)** Repeats.
(ii) Repeats with handsigns.	**(ii)** Repeats with handsigns.
(iii) Sings short phrase using pitch names.	**(iii)** Repeats, but with thinking voice, and showing handsigns.
(iv) Shows a short phrase with handsigns.	**(iv)** Repeats with singing voice only.

In performing these exercises it is essential to change the pitch of **soh** (and therefore of **me**), from time to time.

16 c Improvising. Based on a given rhythm-phrase (e.g. ♫ ♩ ♫ ♩) ask individual children to improvise melodic phrases using **soh** and **me** only. All possibilities should be investigated, starting on **me** as well as on **soh**, and encouraging the children to use handsigns.

FURTHER ▶

16 d Improvising. The teacher (and later individual children) hums an improvised melodic phrase to the minor third (**s–m**) which a child then sings to solfa names (**soh–me**), supported by handsigns.

16 e The Sally Soh and Molly Me game. The teacher greets a child with 'I am Sally Soh' sung on one note. The child responds at the appropriate pitch (with handsigns) 'soh-me, I am Molly Me'. The class sings a chorus:

Sal-ly Soh and Mol-ly Me

The selected child chooses a friend and sings 'I am Molly Me' using the same **me** pitch. The friend, first singing (with handsigns) **me–soh**, responds with 'I am Sally Soh' sung at the related **soh** pitch. The class now sings the chorus:

Mol-ly Me and Sal-ly Soh

The game continues to include other individuals. The pitch of **soh** should be changed from time to time.

☆ **Refer Reading Sheet 14**

Skill/Concept

17 Compound time: feeling and recognising compound time patterns (aural).

Suggested songs/rhymes

5   Chop, chop, choppety chop!
8   To market
40 Snowman, snowman
79 I'm a little Dutchgirl
87 Oats and beans

▷ Children's knowledge of traditional rhymes will
provide a further source of compound time
patterns, e.g. 'Jack and Jill', 'Hickory, dickory, dock'.

Teaching ideas

> ▷ Although songs of simple time pattern (e.g. $\frac{2}{4}$ ♩ ♫ | ♩ 𝄾)
> and compound time pattern (e.g. $\frac{6}{8}$ ♫♫ ♩. | ♩ ♪ ♩.) will have
> been experienced, up to this stage skill and concept development
> has been confined to simple time. Compound time does not
> require the children to assimilate aurally a new rhythmic
> dimension since the speech and poetry patterns of the English
> language (and therefore of English songs and rhymes) are
> frequently rooted in compound rhythm. Because of this, related
> aural skills should be grasped easily.

KEY ▶

17 **a** Movement. Give the children experience of skipping to songs and rhymes which use compound time patterns.

17 **b** Movement. Ask the children (while standing) to sway or swing to the pulse of a compound time song. At a given signal they change to skipping (♩ ♪ ♩ ♪).

17 **c** Sing known songs or chant rhymes, using compound time patterns. After each phrase has been sung/spoken, repeat it – tapping the rhythm only.

17 **d** The children tap a steady pulse on the knees and chant the words 'skipping, skipping' (♩ ♪ ♩ ♪) and 'galloping, galloping' (♫♫ ♫♫).

17 **e** **(i)** Chant the rhyme 'Chop, chop, choppety chop!' to a tapped pulse and repeat, tapping the rhythm.

   (ii) Ask the children to tap the rhythm as they speak the word 'choppety', noting how many taps the word requires.

   (iii) As the children tap and speak the rhyme again, the teacher plays the rhythm of 'choppety' on an instrument whenever the word occurs.

Skill/Concept

18 Pitch: introduction of *lah* with handsign: *l–s–m* (aural).

Suggested songs/rhymes

Songs featuring *l–s–m* intervals

14 Snail, snail
16 Round and round
25 Tick-tock, tick-tock, see my clock
38 Here is the beehive
70 Rat-a-tat-tat!
80 Starlight, star bright

Songs featuring *m–l* interval

15 Rain, rain, go away!
17 Tap, tap, tap!
18 What shall we do?
69 Little Sally Saucer

Teaching ideas

KEY ▶

18 **a** (i) The class sings the first phrase of 'Tick-tock, tick-tock, see my clock'. The children then hum the melody and listen to its pitch contour; this may be emphasised visually by finger-drawing in the air. What do they notice about the pitch contour? The teacher sings the extract to pitch names with supporting handsigns, as follows:

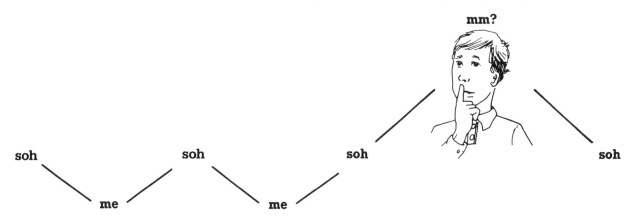

The children imitate.

The teacher repeats, asking the class to smile when the new note is heard. 'What is the pitch name for our smiling note? It is called "lah", with this handsign.' (Show handsign.)

(ii) Work with other phrases from the *Suggested songs* (l–s–m only) which incorporate the new note.

> ▷ With the introduction of **lah**, improvising and exercises using three notes (**l–s–m**) become more complex because there are now three intervals instead of one. The new intervals will need a great deal of practice, both aural and reading (but **l–m** descending is not a feature of the *Key Stage 1* course).

18 b When the children have practised making the new handsign shape (see *Teaching idea* **16 a**), the teacher is recommended to work with *Teaching idea* **16 b** using **U20–U25**. NB The **m–l** leap is not yet used in these examples.

> Examples for the teacher
> **U20** s–l–s
> **U21** s–m–s–l
> **U22** s–s–l–s
> **U23** s–l–s–m
> **U24** m–s–l–l
> **U25** m–s–l–s

> ▷ In the early stages of improvising it is quite usual for some children to sing a melodic phrase in which certain of the singing-names used (solfa) do not accurately correspond to the intervals sung or are wrongly placed. In such cases, the class gives support by humming the melody and the child is encouraged to find the correct singing-name.

18 c Improvising. The teacher invites individual children to improvise melodic phrases using either **soh** and **me**, or **soh** and **lah**; every opportunity should be taken to emphasise the way in which **me** is lower (relative to **soh**) and **lah** is higher. The children should be encouraged to use handsigns, and to start on **me** or **lah** as well as on **soh**.

> ▷ **Remember:** When improvising, change the pitch of **soh** from time to time (with consequent changes to **me** and **lah**).

18 d **(i)** Sing known songs featuring the **m–l** interval (perfect 4th).

(ii) The teacher sings this new interval with pitch names and supporting handsigns. The children repeat.

(iii) The teacher sings short phrases (**U26–U30**) containing the new interval, supported by handsigns. The children repeat each phrase, also using handsigns.

> Examples for the teacher
> **U26** s–m–l–s
> **U27** s–m–l–s–m
> **U28** s–m–l–l
> **U29** m–l–m–l–s
> **U30** s–l–s–m–l

FURTHER ▶

18 e Improvising. Construct the 'human keyboard'. This requires three singers (or small groups) in a row, each responsible for one note: **lah**, **soh** or **me**. The 'player' shows the keyboard a phrase using handsigns. The 'keyboard' sings after the phrase has been shown. It might be helpful if each 'note' of the 'human keyboard' wore a label displaying **lah**, **soh** or **me**, as appropriate.

☆ **Refer Reading Sheet 15**

Skill/Concept

19 Compound time: the pattern of three notes to one pulse, using rhythm names (*ti-ti-ti/tai*); introducing rhythm notation (⊓ ⌐.) and the rest (*z.*).

Suggested songs/rhymes

5   Chop, chop, choppety chop!
6   Twiddle-di-dee
23 Jack-in-the-box
52 Hush, my dear
78 Hammering here

Teaching ideas

> ▷ Compound time is introduced in a similar way to simple time, i.e. based on the pulse.

KEY ▶

19 **a**   The teacher is referred to the *Teaching ideas* used for introducing simple time concepts. The *KEY Teaching ideas* for Skills/Concepts **11** and **12** are suitable and necessary for introducing compound time concepts.

19 **b**   Use a group of children to construct rhythm-phrases of 4-beat length for the class to read with rhythm names (**tai**/**ti-ti-ti**); for example:

tai   ti-ti-ti   tai   (mm)

(A large ball could be used to represent the dot needed for **tai** and its rest.)

☆ **Refer Reading Sheet 16**

> ▷ When the beat is divided in three in this way, the rhythms resulting are described as being in **compound time.** When the beat is divided in two (as in the ⁴⁄₄ rhythms already experienced) the rhythm is described as being in **simple time.**

19 **c**   The teacher is referred to the *Teaching idea* **12** **f** when using compound rhythm cards. In addition, the following game may be played. Ask a child to choose a rhythm card and to speak the rhythm which is unseen by the class. Another child:

(**i**) constructs the phrase with rhythm-people; or

(**ii**) finds the matching card; or

(**iii**) writes the phrase on the board.

The class checks the result.

19 d   Improvising. As for **19 c**, but an individual improvises the 4-beat
phrase by tapping or speaking rhythm names.

19 e   The children read from the board **U31–U35.** Alternatively, the teacher
taps the rhythm, the children speak it to rhythm names and then write
the rhythm, or construct it with lollipop sticks.

Skill/Concept

20   Phrase: feeling, recognising and counting phrases.

Suggested songs/rhymes

20   Rain on the green grass (*2/3 phrases*)
22   Bells in the steeple (*2 phrases*)
23   Jack-in-the-box ⎱ (*1 phrase*)
28   Here we go ⎰
35   Engine, engine (*4 phrases*)
39   Bow, wow, wow! ⎱ (*4 phrases*)
44   See my wellingtons ⎰
49   Pitter patter (*2 phrases*)
51   Once a man fell in a well (*4 phrases*)
71   Tick-tock, tick-tock, tell the time (*2 phrases*)
93   Oh, there are four seasons (*2 phrases*)

▷ With some songs, the phrase length is a matter
for interpretation.

Teaching ideas

KEY ▶

20 **a**   Movement. Find one movement for the duration of each phrase. How
many times is the movement performed as the song is sung? (e.g. Sing
'Engine, engine'; draw a large wheel in the air for each phrase.)

20 **b**   The teacher is referred to the *Teaching ideas* used for introducing an
awareness of phrase length in *Skill/Concept* 3 ; these are also useful for
counting phrases.

20 **c**   With the teacher indicating the pulse, the children sing the first phrase
of a song, use the thinking voice for the second phrase, sing the third
phrase, think the fourth phrase, etc.

20 **d**   Ask the children to sing a familiar song and at the same time to draw
with the finger on the floor, or in the air, a new number for each phrase
they hear, beginning with number 1. The final number will give them
the total number of phrases.

> ▷ It is possible that some children might begin to make
> comparisons between phrases they have identified. When this
> happens naturally, the teacher should pursue the ideas which
> emerge, but without attempting any detailed analysis at this stage.

20 **e**   Ask a child to draw on the board a rainbow shape for each melodic
phrase of a song, as it is sung by the class (e.g. ⌒). In a similar
way, the class may trace this shape through the air as they sing. The
number of rainbows on the board will show the number of phrases in the
song.

Skill/Concept

21 Melody: constructing melodic phrases by combining pitch and rhythm elements, and writing them by combining pitch and rhythm symbols (rhythm-solfa) – simple time only.

Rhythm-solfa: The value of rhythm-solfa is the clear way in which it combines rhythm and pitch elements as a representation of complete melodic phrases. It provides the opportunity for much-needed practice for readers in the early stages. Rhythm or pitch elements may be emphasised according to need.

Teaching ideas

KEY▶

21 a Improvising. To a given simple rhythm phrase (e.g. ♩ ♫♩ ♩) ask individual children to improvise a melodic phrase using **lah, soh** and **me** (supported by handsigns). The children may use the rising interval **m–l**.

The teacher writes the rhythm-phrase on the board, for example:

♩ ♫♩ ♩

and from the improvised melodic phrase received, writes the pitch symbol under the rhythm symbol;
for example:

♩ ♫♩ ♩
s m m l s

> ▷ Note heads are used for rhythm-solfa notation.

The teacher tells the class that this form of notation is called **rhythm-solfa**. Individual children continue to improvise vocal phrases to the same rhythm, and to write them on the board themselves in rhythm-solfa.

☆ **Refer Reading Sheets 17 and 18**

21 b Different rhythm-phrases may now be used. The teacher might find rhythm cards helpful for this.

> ▷ At this stage, simple time rhythms only are used for reading and writing rhythm-solfa.

FURTHER ▶

21 c Instruments. A child may wish to play his/her improvised piece on a melodic instrument, e.g. xylophone, chime-bars. Make sure the child understands which notes represent the solfa names, and that prior to playing, s/he can sing the example accurately. Do not ask the child to read and play simultaneously.

▷ When children use keyboard instruments or pitched percussion (xylophone, glockenspiel, etc.) to perform melodies using **s–m–l**, the following pitch groupings are recommended:

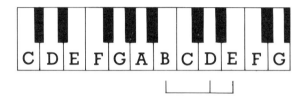

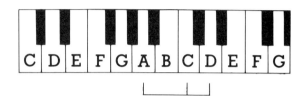

21 d Arrange for the children to take home examples of their own written improvisations which they have shown they can perform vocally with accuracy and confidence.

21 e **U36–U38** are for reading practice with rhythm-solfa. Having written a chosen example on the board, ask the children to consider the rhythm first, speaking, then tapping the rhythm shown. When this is secure, use handsigns to remind the children of the **l–s–m** pitch relationship, and finally ask them to read rhythm and pitch together to obtain the melody. **U36**, **U37** and **U38** are probably known melodies; ask the children to identify the song, and then sing it to the words.

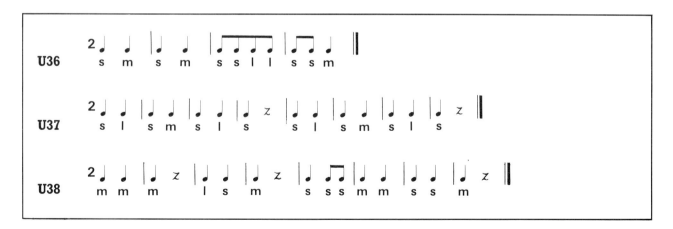

Song collection: alphabetic index

Song collection: analytical index

No	Title	Tone-set	Time signature	Rhythm-set	Game/Actions
1	Hello, how are you?	s–m	2/4	♩ ♫	
2	Cobbler, cobbler	rhyme	2/4	♩ ♫ 𝄽	Actions
3	Jelly on a plate	rhyme	2/4	♩ ♫ 𝄽	
4	Mice, mice	rhyme	2/4	♩ ♫ 𝄽	
5	Chop, chop, choppety chop!	rhyme	6/8	♩. ♫♫	
6	Twiddle-di-dee	rhyme	6/8	♩. ♪ ♩	Game
7	One potato	rhyme	6/8	♩. ♪ 𝄽.	
8	To market	rhyme	6/8	♩. ♪ ♫♫	
9	I, I, me oh my!	s–m	2/4	♩ ♫	Game
10	See-saw	s–m	2/4	♩ ♫	Actions
11	Cuckoo! Cherry tree	s–m	3/4	♩ 𝅗𝅥 ♫.	Game
12	Pears for pies	s–m	6/8	♩. ♪ 𝄽 ♪ 𝄽.	
13	Rap-a tap-a	l–s–m	2/4	♩ ♫	Game
14	Snail, snail	l–s–m	2/4	♩ ♫	
15	Rain, rain, go away!	l–s–m	2/4	♩ ♫	Game
16	Round and round	l–s–m	2/4	♩ 𝄽	Game
17	Tap, tap, tap!	l–s–m	4/4	♩ ♫ 𝄽	
18	What shall we do	l–s–m	3/8	♩. ♪ ♫♫	

No	Title	Tone-set	Time signature	Rhythm-set	Game/Actions
19	Roll up! Here's the fair	s–m–d	2/4	♩ ♫	
20	Rain on the green grass	s–d	2/4	♩ ♫ 𝄽	
21	I see you	s–m–d	2/4	♩ ♫ 𝄽	
22	Bells in the steeple	s–m–d	3/4	♩ 𝅝	
23	Jack-in-the-box	s–m–d	6/8	♩. ♫ 𝄽.	Actions
24	Can you tap your fingers?	s–m–d	6/8	♩. ♩. ♪	Actions
25	Tick-tock, tick-tock, see my clock	l–s–m–d	2/4	♩ 𝄽	
26	This is how a drummer-boy/girl	s–m–r	2/4	♩ ♫ 𝄽	Actions
27	Rabbit in the hollow	m–r–d	2/4	♩ ♫ 𝄽	Game
28	Here we go	m–r–d	2/4	♩ ♫ 𝄽	
29	Make the porridge in a pan	m–r–d	6/8	♩. ♩ ♪	Dance
30	Listen, listen, here I come	s–m–r–d	2/4	♩ ♫	Game
31	Little Arabella Miller	s–m–r–d	2/4	♫	
32	I have a dog	s–m–r–d	2/4	♩ ♫ 𝄽	
33	Lots of rosy apples	s–m–r–d	2/4	♩ ♫ 𝄽	Game
34	Who is that I see?	s–m–r–d	4/4	♩ ♫ 𝄽	
35	Engine, engine	l–s–m–r–d	2/4	♩ ♫ 𝄽	
36	Tom cats, alley cats	l–s–m–r–d	2/4	♩ ♫ 𝄽	

No	Title	Tone-set	Time signature	Rhythm-set	Game/Actions
37	Who has the penny?	l-s-m-r-d	2/4	♪ ♩	Game
38	Here is the beehive	l-s-m-r-d	4/4	♩ ♩ 𝄽	
39	Bow, wow, wow!	l-s-m-r-d	4/4	♩ ♩ 𝄽	Game
40	Snowman, snowman	l-s-m-r-d	6/8	♩. ♪ ♫	
41	A goblin lives in our house	m-r-d-l,	2/4	♩ ♩ 𝄾 ♪	
42	Chuffa, chuffa, chuff!	d-l,-s,	2/4	♩ ♩ 𝄽	
43	Hickety tickety	d-l,-s,	6/8	♩. ♪ ♫	Game
44	See my wellingtons	m-r-d-l,-s,	2/4	♩ ♩	
45	Ding, dong	m-r-d-s,	3/4	𝅗𝅥. ♩	
46	Tell me, shepherdess	m-r-d-s,	2/4	♩ ♩ 𝄽	
47	Pease pudding hot	f-m-r-d	2/4	♩ ♩ 𝄽	
48	Down the hill	f-m-r-d	2/4	♩ ♩	
49	Pitter patter	s-f-m-r-d	2/4	♩ ♩ 𝄽	
50.	Clip, clop	s-f-m-r-d	2/4	♩ ♩	
51	Once a man fell in a well	s-f-m-r-d	2/4	♩ ♩ 𝄽	
52	Hush, my dear	s-f-m-r-d	6/8	♩. ♪ ♫	
53	Glowing candle-light	l-s-f-m-r-d	2/4	♩ ♩ 𝄽	
54	Pancake Tuesday	l-s-f-m-r-d	4/4	𝅗𝅥 ♩ ♪ ♩	

No	Title	Tone-set	Time signature	Rhythm-set	Game/Actions
55	Willum he had seven sons	f-m-r-d-t,-l,	2/4	(rhythm notation)	Actions
56	Little Johnny dances	f-m-r-d-t,-l,	2/4	(rhythm notation)	Actions
57	Pee, Pee, Pollyanna	s-f-m-r-d-t,-l,-s,	2/4 /8	(rhythm notation)	Game
58	Apples, peaches, pears and plums	rhyme	2/4	(rhythm notation)	
59	Piggy on the railway	rhyme	2/4	(rhythm notation)	
60	Here sits the Lord Mayor	rhyme	2/4	(rhythm notation)	Actions
61	Tick-tack-too	rhyme	2/4	(rhythm notation)	
62	Zinty tinty	rhyme	6/8	(rhythm notation)	
63	An elephant goes like this	rhyme	6/8	(rhythm notation)	Actions
64	I wiggle my fingers	rhyme	6/8	(rhythm notation)	Actions
65	Hey! Hey! Look at me!	s-m	2/4	(rhythm notation)	Game
66	Teddy Bear, Teddy Bear	s-m	2/4	(rhythm notation)	Actions
67	Here I come	s-m	2/4	(rhythm notation)	Game
68	Let us make a ring	l-s-m	2/4	(rhythm notation)	Game
69	Little Sally Saucer	l-s-m	2/4	(rhythm notation)	Game
70	Rat-a-tat-tat!	l-s-m	4/4	(rhythm notation)	Game
71	Tick-tock, tick-tock, tell the time	s-m-d	2/4	(rhythm notation)	

No	Title	Tone-set	Time signature	Rhythm-set	Game/Actions
72	Little pony, gallop home	m–r–d	2/4	*(rhythm notation)*	
73	Hands are cold	m–r–d	6/8	*(rhythm notation)*	Actions
74	My little baby	s–m–r–d	2/4	*(rhythm notation)*	
75	Sleep, baby, sleep	s–m–r–d	2/4	*(rhythm notation)*	
76	Fox is running	s–m–r–d	2/4	*(rhythm notation)*	Game
77	Bought me a cat	s–m–r–d	2/4	*(rhythm notation)*	
78	Hammering here	s–m–r–d	6/8	*(rhythm notation)*	
79	I'm a little Dutchgirl	s–m–r–d	6/8	*(rhythm notation)*	Game
80	Starlight, star bright	s–m–r–d	2/4	*(rhythm notation)*	
81	Here comes a bluebird	l–s–m–r–d	4/4	*(rhythm notation)*	Game
82	Button you must wander	l–s–m–r–d	2/4	*(rhythm notation)*	Game
83	See the Indian chief	m–d–l,–s,	2/4	*(rhythm notation)*	
84	Down came a lady	m–d–l,–s,	2/4	*(rhythm notation)*	Game
85	Sally go round the sun	f–m–r–d	6/8	*(rhythm notation)*	Game
86	Go and tell Aunt Nancy	s–f–m–r–d	2/4	*(rhythm notation)*	
87	Oats and beans	s–f–m–r–d	6/8	*(rhythm notation)*	Game
88	Fair Rosa was a pretty child	l–s–f–m–r–d	2/4	*(rhythm notation)*	Game
89	We're Mother Piggy's piggy piglets	l–s–f–m–r–d	3/4	*(rhythm notation)*	Game

No	Title	Tone-set	Time signature	Rhythm-set	Game/Actions
90	High on a leaf	l–s–f–m–r–d	$\frac{2}{4}$	♩ ♪. ♪ ♫ 𝅗𝅥	
91	What shall we play?	l–s–f–m–r–d	$\frac{2}{4}$	♩ ♩ ♫ ♩♫ 𝅗𝅥	
92	One little candle	m–r–d–t,–l,	$\frac{4}{4}$	♩ 𝅗𝅥 ♫ 𝅝	
93	Oh, there are four seasons	m–r–d–t,–s,	$\frac{3}{4}$	♩ ♩ 𝅗𝅥	
94	Farmer Higgs	m–r–d–t,–l,–s,	$\frac{2}{4}$	♫ ♩ ♩	
95	Alice the camel	m–r–d–t,–l,–s,	$\frac{4}{4}$	♪. ♩ ♪♩ ♪ ♫ ♩ ♩ z	Game
96	Have you seen the muffin man?	m–r–d–t,–l,–s,	$\frac{2}{4}$	♩ ♫♩ ♫ z	Game
97	I walked to the top of the hill	f–m–r–d–t,–l,–s,	$\frac{4}{4}$	♩. ♩ ♫ 𝅗𝅥.	

Song collection

Songs **1**–**57** provide core material for use with the *Course programme*.
Songs **58**–**97** provide additional repertoire which can be used to
broaden experience. (See Song collection notes on pages 11–12)

1

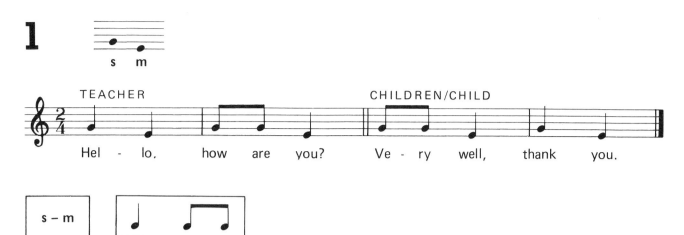

A pleasant and musical idea to start the day or music session.

Further idea:
The teacher, or a child, improvises melodies for other words e.g.
(a) Good morning everyone.
(b) Goodbye, see you all tomorrow.

2

Traditional children's action song

Cob - bler, cob - bler, mend my shoe. Get it done by half past two;

One, two, lit - tle toes are peep - ing through. Please mend it do!

Activities

Suggested actions

Cobbler, cobbler, mend my shoe. ——————— Bang one fist on another

Get it done by half past two; ——————— Wagging pointed finger

One, two, ——————— Count on fingers

little toes are ——————— Point to toes

peeping through ——————— Peep through finger 'spectacles'

Please mend it do. Z ——————— Hands turned upwards in pleading gesture

(All to a pulse)

☆

3

Traditional skipping rhyme

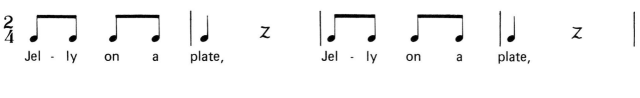

Jel - ly on a plate, Jel - ly on a plate,

Wib - ble wob - ble, wib - ble wob - ble, Jel - ly on a plate.

2 Sausage in the pan,
Sausage in the pan,
Turn it over, turn it over,
Sausage in the pan.

3 Ghostie in the house,
Ghostie in the house,
Turn him out, turn him out,
Ghostie in the house.

4

Mice, mice, Eat - ing up the rice.

Nib - ble, nib - ble, nib - ble, nib - ble, Nice, nice, nice.

65

5

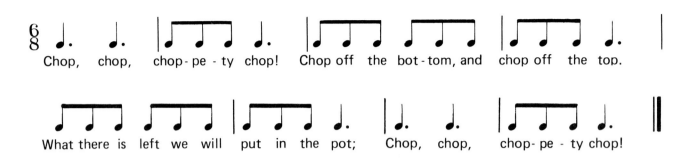

Chop, chop, chop-pe-ty chop! Chop off the bot-tom, and chop off the top.

What there is left we will put in the pot; Chop, chop, chop-pe-ty chop!

6

Traditional

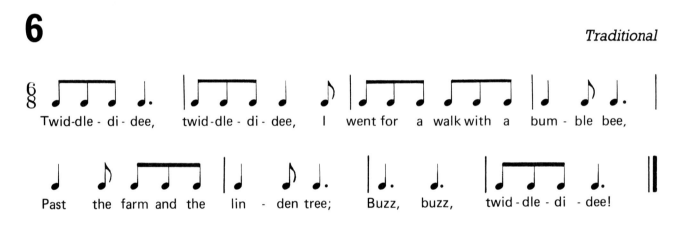

Twid-dle-di-dee, twid-dle-di-dee, I went for a walk with a bum-ble bee,

Past the farm and the lin - den tree; Buzz, buzz, twid-dle-di-dee!

7

Traditional dip rhyme

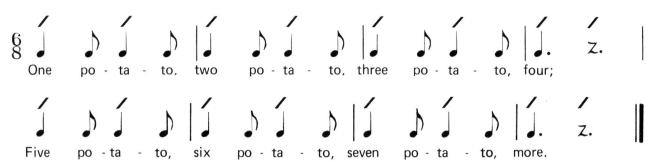

One po-ta-to, two po-ta-to, three po-ta-to, four;
Five po-ta-to, six po-ta-to, seven po-ta-to, more.

Activities

Game

The children stand in a circle, each person with clenched fists held out in front. The rhyme is chanted rhythmically as the leader passes round the circle to each child in turn, tapping every fist with his/her own, in time to the pulse. (∕)

The child whose fist is tapped on the word 'more' places that fist behind his/her back – and the rhyme starts again.

The last child remaining with an untouched fist is 'chosen'.

8

Traditional

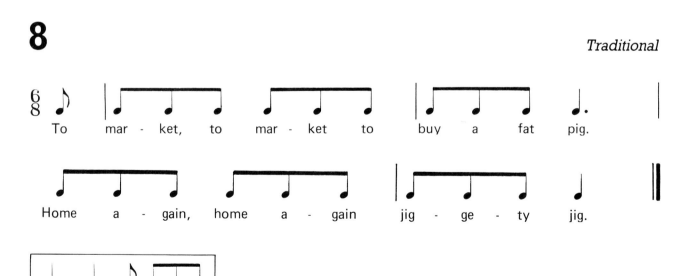

To mar-ket, to mar-ket to buy a fat pig.
Home a-gain, home a-gain jig-ge-ty jig.

2 To market, to market to buy a fat hog.
   Home again, home again jiggety jog.

I,   I,   me oh my!   How   I   love that   cher - ry   pie!

Activities

Game

Pass a ball round the circle to the pulse of
the song. Whoever has the ball on the
word 'pie' sings the song, substituting a
new pie, e.g. 'apple pie'.

The new version is then sung by all as the
ball is passed round the circle again.

10

See - saw,   up and down,   in   the   sky and   on   the ground.

Activities

Suggested actions to mark the pulse

(a) sway side to side;

(b) sway forwards and backwards;

(c) bend the knees, straighten the knees;

(d) hold a partner's hands, and go up and
down together or alternately.

11

s   m

Children's game (Britain)

Cuc - koo!   Cher - ry   tree,   Catch the   ball,   Throw to   me.
(Roll)   (Roll)

s – m

Activities

Game

Two children stand in the centre of a circle of children, one with a ball; this child sings the song. At 'Catch', s/he throws/rolls the ball to his/her partner and asks for its return.

Further idea

Children as before. One child chooses a large/middle/small sized ball/bean-bag. The two children stand arm's length apart. The song is sung as before. If the ball/bag is caught, each partner takes a step back, and the song and the catching is repeated until the partners reach the the children behind them in the circle. The game is then repeated with another two children. If the ball/bag is dropped, that partner is 'out' and a new one is chosen.

Variant

Cuckoo! Where are you?	(1)
Cuckoo! I am here.	(2)
Peek-a-boo! I see you.	(3)

One child hides as another sits with closed eyes. The latter sings question (1). The hidden child replies (2). The first child points to the direction of the answer, singing (3), then opens his/her eyes.

12

Traditional seller's cry (London)

Pears for pies, Come feast your eyes! Ri - pest pears of

ev - 'ry size, Who'll buy? Who'll buy?

2 Beans for stew,
   So good for you!
   Chase away the colds and 'flu,
   Who'll buy? Who'll buy?

3 Plums so sweet,
   A fam'ly treat!
   Juicy, and so nice to eat,
   Who'll buy? Who'll buy?

13

Rap - a tap - a, rap - a too, Mis - ter Cob - bler mend my shoe.

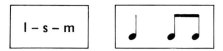

2 Mend my shoe, and when it's done
   I can walk and jump and run.

14

l   s   m

Traditional children's song (Cornwall, England)

Snail,   snail,   snail,   snail,   Go   a - round,   and   round,   and   round.

l – s – m

Activities

Game
Children form a line, holding hands.
One end is stationary; the player at the
other end leads the line around in a
sweeping circle, slowly winding everyone
into the spiral shape of a snail shell.

☆

15

l   s   m

Traditional children's song (Britain)

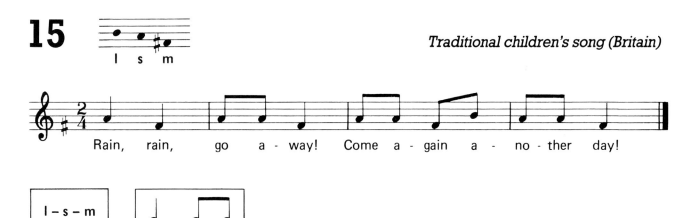

Rain,   rain,   go   a - way!   Come   a - gain   a - no - ther   day!

l – s – m

2 Sunshine's here to stay.
Now we can go out to play.

71

16

l   s   m

Round   and   round   the   mill   goes   round;

As   it   turns   the   corn   is   ground.

Activities

Game

The children make a circle with a chosen child as the miller in the centre. Outside the circle, two children play the parts of the farmer and the baker. The farmer sells his corn to the miller. The miller winds a handle, and the circle turns to grind the corn as the song is sung. Finally, the miller sells his flour to the baker.

☆

17

l   s   m

Tap, tap, tap!   Who is that?   On - ly the wit - ch's big black cat.

(Whisper) Sh! Sh! Sh!   Who is there?   On - ly a ghost be - hind the stair.

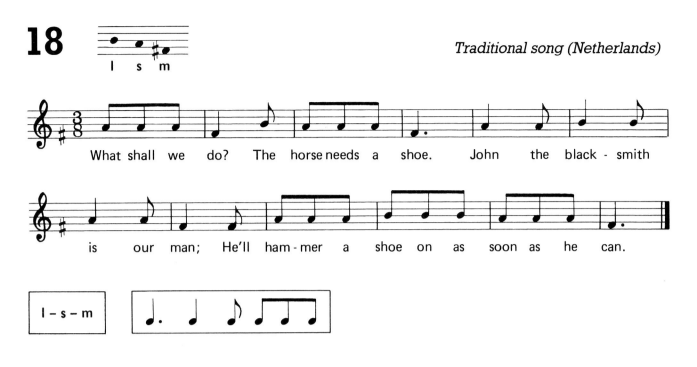

18 Traditional song (Netherlands)

l s m

What shall we do? The horse needs a shoe. John the black - smith

is our man; He'll ham - mer a shoe on as soon as he can.

l – s – m

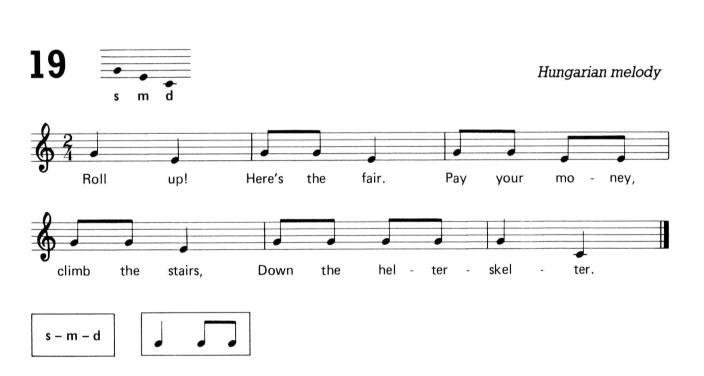

19 Hungarian melody

s m d

Roll up! Here's the fair. Pay your mo - ney,

climb the stairs, Down the hel - ter - skel - ter.

s – m – d

20

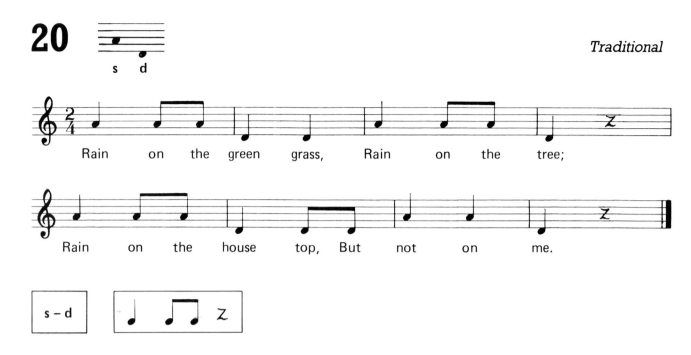

Traditional

Rain on the green grass, Rain on the tree;

Rain on the house top, But not on me.

s – d

21

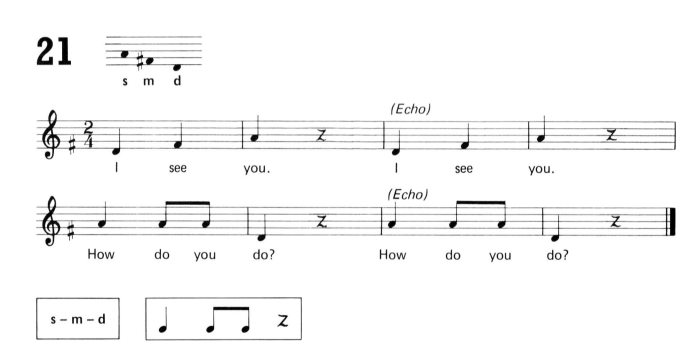

(Echo)

I see you. I see you.

(Echo)

How do you do? How do you do?

s – m – d

2 Can you ride? I've never tried.

3 Can you run? Yes, it is fun.

4 Can you fly? Yes, so good-bye.

22

Children's song (Sweden)

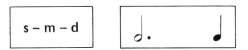

23

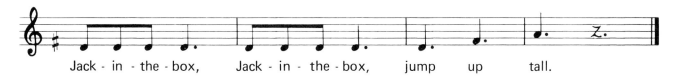

Activities

Actions
The children will enjoy playing the part of
Jack-in-the-box. The second half of the
song in particular gives the opportunity to
encourage rhythmic movements.

Can you tap your fin - gers? *(Action:Tap   tap   tap   tap.)*

Yes,   we can,   yes,   we can.   Well   done!   Well   done!

Activities

Actions
The children will enjoy making the appropriate actions to the following verses.

2 Can you tap your shoulders?

3 Can you wave your hands high?

4 Can you stand up slowly?

5 Can you tip-toe quietly?

6 Can you sit down gently?

7 Can you clap a loud pulse?

8 Own verse.

25

l s m d

Tick - tock, tick - tock, see my clock.

Tick - tock, tick - tock, *twelve o' clock.

★ Change the hour as appropriate

26

s m r

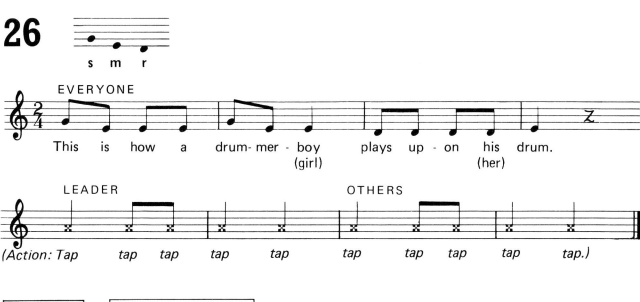

EVERYONE

This is how a drum-mer - boy plays up - on his drum.
(girl) (her)

LEADER OTHERS

(Action: Tap tap tap tap tap tap tap tap tap tap.)

Activities

This song provides an introduction to feeling a pulse through body sounds such as tapping knees, or shoulders.

The song may also be used to give experience of tapped 4-beat rhythm-phrases:
(a) using invented rhythm language (e.g. 'tacky, tacky, tacky, too');
(b) by tapped improvising;
(c) using standard rhythm language.

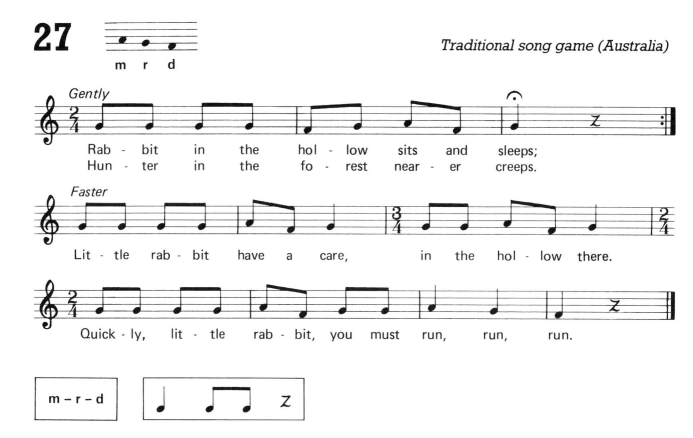

27

Traditional song game (Australia)

Gently

Rab - bit   in   the   hol - low   sits   and   sleeps;
Hun - ter   in   the   fo - rest   near - er   creeps.

Faster

Lit - tle   rab - bit   have   a   care,   in   the   hol - low   there.

Quick - ly,   lit - tle   rab - bit,   you   must   run,   run,   run.

m – r – d

Activities

Game

The children sit in a circle, facing inwards, with a space between each child. One child is the rabbit, crouching quietly in the centre; another child is the hunter, stalking around the outside of the circle. On the words 'Quickly, little rabbit' the hunter enters the circle to chase, and to try to catch, the rabbit. The rabbit immediately runs out of the circle and round the outside – returning to the centre of the circle via the same opening. The hunter may not re-enter the circle.

28

Here   we   go,   soft   and   slow,   Mak - ing   pat - terns   in   the   snow.

m – r – d

2   Oh, how nice, once or twice,
Slipping, sliding on the ice!

29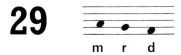

Make the por - ridge in a pan, Ma - ry Ann, Ma - ry Ann.

Make it a - ny way you can, Ma - ry Ann, Ma - ry Ann.

2 Pour yourself a cup of tea,
Ann-Marie, Ann-Marie.
One for you and one for me,
Ann-Marie, Ann-Marie.

3 Cook a cake for us to eat,
Marguerite, Marguerite.
It will be a birthday treat,
Marguerite, Marguerite.

Activities

Dance
The children form three separate circles
without holding hands, each circle
representing a verse of the song. The
members of each circle in turn skip to the
centre, tap the character's name on their
hands (end of first phrase), skip backwards
to their places, and again tap the
character's name on their hands (end of
second phrase). As each circle is
performing its verse, the other two circles
skip clockwise (first phrase), tap the name
– then skip anticlockwise (second phrase),
and tap the name.

Lis - ten, lis - ten, here I come. Some - one spe - cial gets the drum.

Activities

Game

The children stand in a circle, facing outwards. A chosen child walks the pulse, and on an instrument (drum, tambourine) taps to the pulse or to the rhythm of the song, as s/he sings. The child walks the inside of the circle, close to the other children. When s/he stops on the last note of the song, the nearest child turns and takes the instrument. The game is then repeated.

(Different ends of the beater might be used, according to whether the pulse or the rhythm has been chosen – e.g. large head of beater for the pulse, small head of beater for the rhythm.)

31

Traditional

Lit - tle A - ra - bel - la Mil - ler Had a wool - ly ca - ter - pil - lar.
First she put it on her mo - ther, Then up - on her ba - by bro - ther.

All said, 'A - ra - bel - la Mil - ler, Take a - way that ca - ter - pil - lar.'

32

Traditional rhyme (England)

I have a *dog and *his name is *Ro - ver;

*He is the one I love the best.

2 When *he is good *he is good all over;
When *he is bad *he is just a pest.

* Encourage children to sing about their own
pets by substituting appropriate words.

33

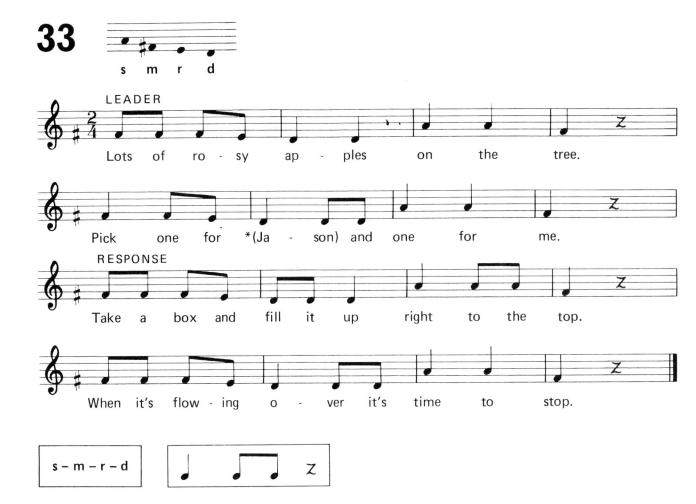

s   m   r   d

LEADER

Lots   of   ro - sy   ap - ples   on   the   tree.

Pick   one   for   *(Ja - son) and   one   for   me.

RESPONSE

Take   a   box   and   fill   it   up   right   to   the   top.

When   it's   flow - ing   o - ver   it's   time   to   stop.

s – m – r – d

Activities

Game

The children stand in any suitable formation
and one child is chosen to start the song.
S/he begins the verse and chooses a child
to continue the song, singing the chosen
child's name* to complete the words. When
all the children have sung to the end of the
verse, the named child begins again . . .

☆

34

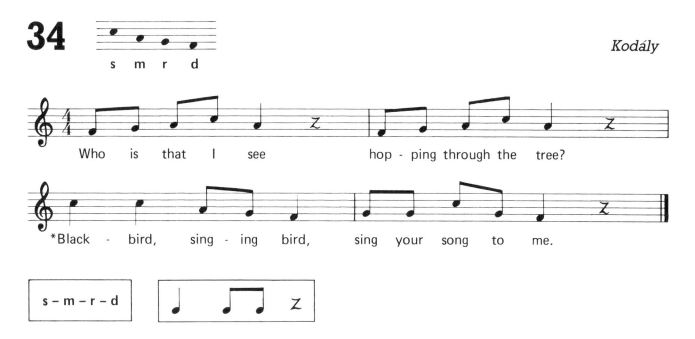

Kodály

s   m   r   d

Who is that I see hop - ping through the tree?

*Black - bird, sing - ing bird, sing your song to me.

s – m – r – d

* The names of other songbirds could be substituted, for example:
robin, greenfinch, sparrow.

35

l   s   m   r   d

En - gine, en - gine, num - ber nine, Run -ning on *Chi - ca - go line,

If she's po - lished, how she'll shine! En - gine, en - gine, num - ber nine.

l – s – m – r – d

2 Engine, engine, number nine,
Running on *Chicago line,
If the train goes off the track,
Do you want your money back?

* Children may substitute a place-name of
their own choice.

36

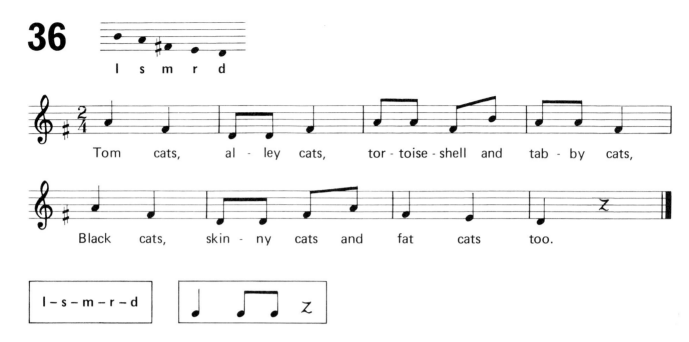

l   s   m   r   d

Tom cats, al - ley cats, tor - toise - shell and tab - by cats,

Black cats, skin - ny cats and fat cats too.

l – s – m – r – d

2 Pet dogs, happy dogs, snappy dogs and
yappy dogs,
Stray dogs, puppy dogs and hot dogs too.

37

─── Activities ───

Game 'Who Has It?'

(1) The teacher improvises melodic phrases in the form of questions. The children answer, if appropriate, using the same melodic phrase. For example: 'Who has a sister?' – 'I have a sister.' 'Who's wearing brown shoes?' – 'I'm wearing brown shoes.'

(2) The teacher has three or four objects (e.g. pencil, penny, rubber). The children close their eyes and hold out their hands. The teacher gives the objects to three or four individuals. The game proceeds as in paragraph (1) above – but this time is played with eyes closed, and the responses are individual.

(3) When confidence is established, a child might be invited to take the role of the teacher, using the above ideas.

☆

Examples of improvised phrases:

l   s   m   r   d

(a)

(b)

(c)

38

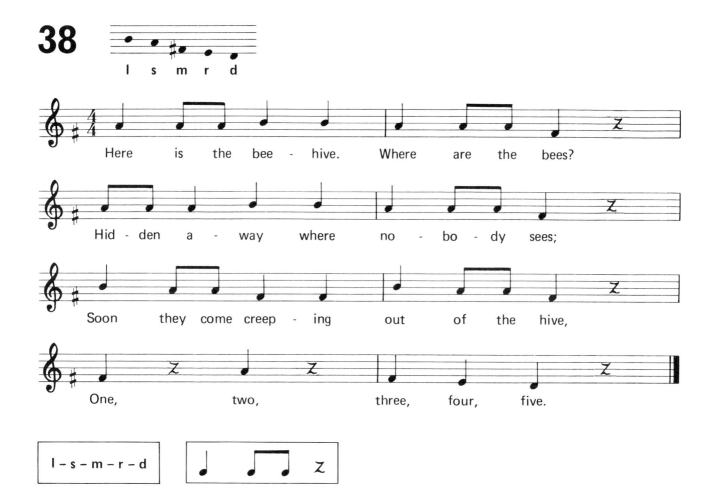

l s m r d

Here is the bee - hive. Where are the bees?

Hid - den a - way where no - bo - dy sees;

Soon they come creep - ing out of the hive,

One, two, three, four, five.

l – s – m – r – d

39

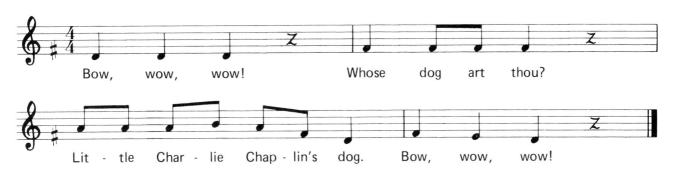

Children's song (England)

l s m r d

Bow, wow, wow!   Whose dog art thou?

Lit - tle Char - lie Chap - lin's dog.   Bow, wow, wow!

l – s – m – r – d

Activities

One child sings the first line of the song to another child of his/her choice. The second child sings the second line, substituting the 'Little Charlie Chaplin's' with his/her personal names. The song is repeated in a similar way when the second child approaches a third child.

Game
The children stand in a circle. They turn to face partners. During the first bar of the song the children gently slap each other's held-up hands, and during the second bar they wag a finger at each other. In the third bar the children move forward in the direction they are facing, passing by their partner's right shoulder – and meeting their new partners in time to slap held-up hands for the fourth bar. The song and the sequence of actions are then repeated.

40

l s m r d

Snow - man, snow - man, can you build a snow - man?

Build him fat and build him tall; give him a push and down he'll fall.

l – s – m – r – d

41

m r d l₁

A gob-lin lives in our house, in our house, in our house; A gob-lin lives in our house all the year round.

Fine

D.C. al Fine*

He bumps and he jumps and he thumps and he stumps.
He knocks and he rocks and he rat-tles at the locks.

m – r – d – l₁

**D.C. al Fine* is an indication to repeat from the beginning and stop at *Fine.*

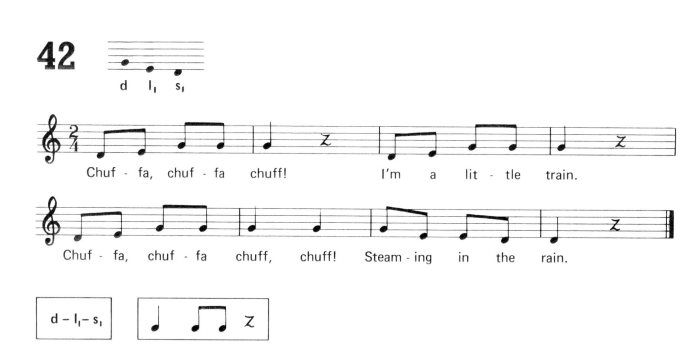

42

d l₁ s₁

Chuf-fa, chuf-fa chuff! I'm a lit-tle train.
Chuf-fa, chuf-fa chuff, chuff! Steam-ing in the rain.

d – l₁ – s₁

2 Puffa, puffa puff! Putting on my brake.
Puffa, puffa, puff, puff! What a noise I make!

43

Children's song (Britain)

LEADER

Hick - e - ty tick - e - ty bum - ble bee, Can you sing your

RESPONSE

name for me? *(Sal - ly A - dams) is my name.

Activities

Game

* When asked the question, the child replies with his/her own name.

  Sing the same tune with the following words:

  Hickety tickety horney cup,
  How many fingers* do I hold up?

* Similarly, when asked the question, the child offers an answer.

☆

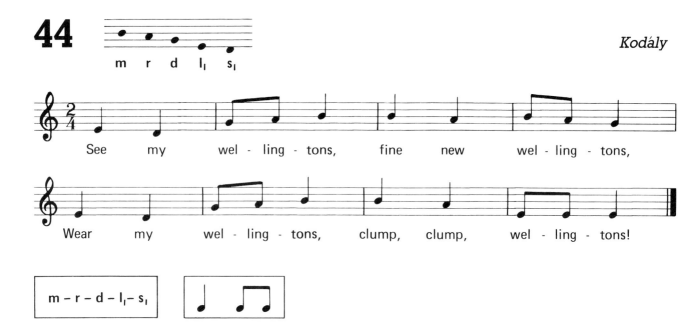

44

Kodály

m r d l₁ s₁

See my wel - ling - tons, fine new wel - ling - tons,

Wear my wel - ling - tons, clump, clump, wel - ling - tons!

m – r – d – l₁ – s₁

2 See my motor car, bright new motor car,
  Drive my motor car, brrm, brrm, motor car.

3 See my pink ice-cream, cold new pink ice-cream,
  Lick my pink ice-cream, yum, yum, pink ice-cream.

4 See my big bass drum, loud new big bass drum,
  Beat my big bass drum, bam, bam, big bass drum.

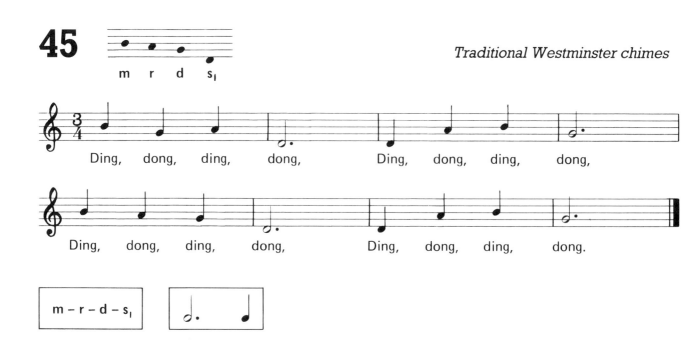

45

Traditional Westminster chimes

m r d s₁

Ding, dong, ding, dong, Ding, dong, ding, dong,

Ding, dong, ding, dong, Ding, dong, ding, dong.

m – r – d – s₁

46

Folk song (Anjou)

m   r   d   s₁

Tell me,   shep - herd - ess   Where   have   you   been?

To   a   hum - ble   sta - ble   Where   a   babe   was   born,

Born   of   Mo - ther   Ma - ry   On   this   hap - py   morn.

m – r – d – s₁

2 Tell me, shepherdess, what did you there?
      Touched his tiny fingers,
      Touched his tiny toes;
      Watched him weeping, sleeping,
      In his swaddling clothes.

3 Tell me, shepherdess, what did you see?
      Angels on the highway,
      Wise men at the door;
      Royal gifts in plenty,
      On the stable floor.

4 Tell me, shepherdess, can we come too?
      Come to Him by starlight,
      Come to Him by love;
      Here is heavenly treasure
      Sent you from above.

47

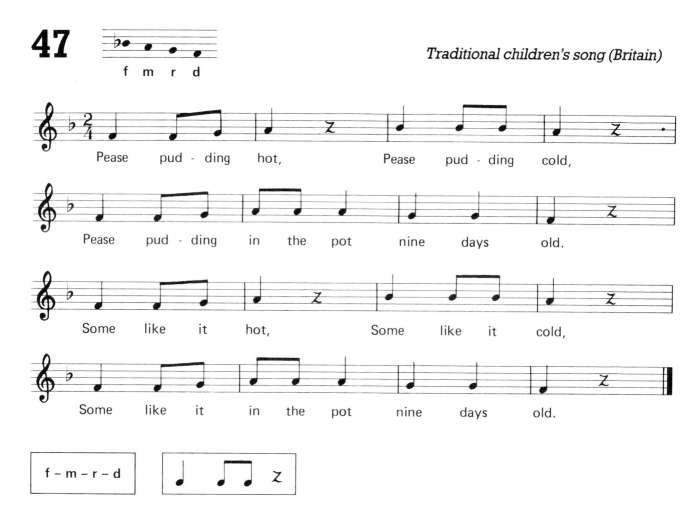

Traditional children's song (Britain)

48

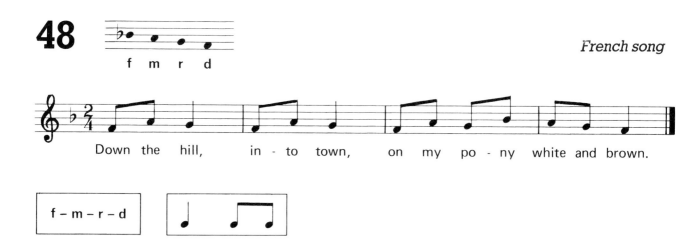

French song

2 Up the lane, trotting back, on my pony glossy black.

3 Through the fields, trot away, on my pony dapple grey.

49

s f m r d

Pit - ter pat - ter, pit - ter pat - ter, Lis - ten to the rain.

Pit - ter pat - ter, pit - ter pat - ter, On the win - dow pane.

2 Splishy sploshy, splishy sploshy,
I am getting wet.
Splishy sploshy, splishy sploshy,
Raindrops on my head.

3 Dripping dropping, dripping dropping,
Water pouring down.
Dripping dropping, dripping dropping,
Hoping we don't drown.

4 (Silence* _____)
Now the rain has stopped.
(Silence* _____)
No more rain to drop.

(*Teacher taps 4 beats, in tempo.)

50

s f m r d

Clip, clop, clip, clop, Off to mar - ket, ne - ver stop.

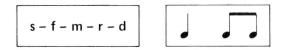

2 Pit, pat, pit, pat,
One big raindrop on my hat.

3 Tip, toe, tip, toe,
Can you hear the daises grow.

4 Lip, tee, lip, tee,
You are 'it' and can't catch me.

5 Chop, chip, chop, chip,
Cut a tree and build a ship.

6 Wick, wack, wick, wack,
See the witch's old black cat.

51

German traditional melody

s f m r d

Once a man fell in a well; Splish, splash, splosh he sound - ed.

If he had not fall - en in He would not have drowned - ed.

s – f – m – r – d

52

British lullaby

s f m r d

TEACHER
Gently lilting

Hush, my dear, the gal - lop - ing men, Ride through the brack - en and
Close your eyes and cry no more, Mum - my has told you

back a - gain. Mum - my will watch her sleep - ing hen, So
that be - fore. Dad - dy's a - sleep in the rock - ing chair, So

CHILDREN
Fine Very fast

close your eyes my dear - ie. Will you be still, my
close your eyes my dear - ie.

D.C. al Fine

fidg - e - ty, fidg - e - ty, fidg - e - ty, fidg - e - ty, fidg - e - ty bairn.

s – f – m – r – d

53

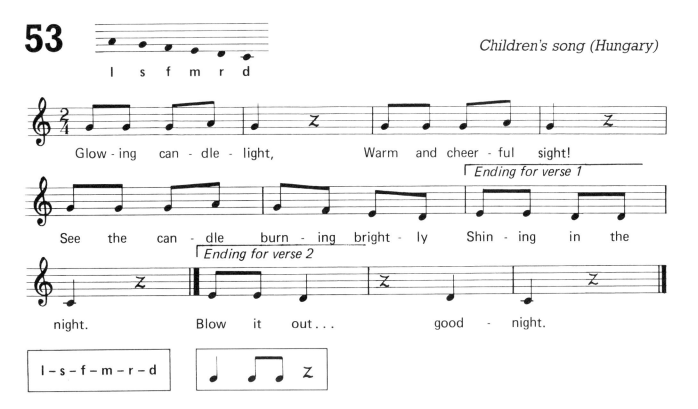

Children's song (Hungary)

l - s - f - m - r - d

2 See the candle-light,
See how tall and bright,
We don't need it while we're sleeping.
Blow it out . . . good-night.

54

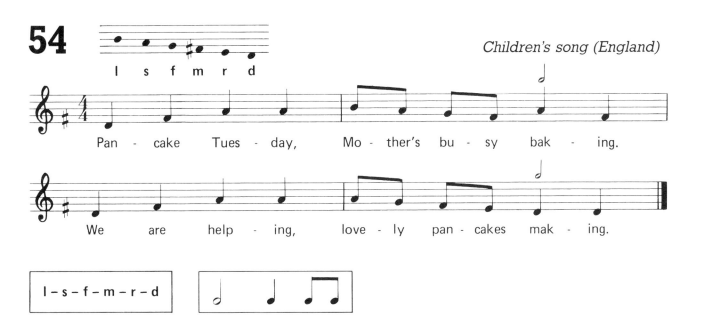

Children's song (England)

l - s - f - m - r - d

2 Mix them up and drop them in the pan.
Toss them up and catch them if you can.

55

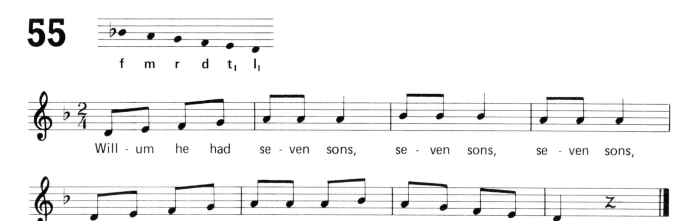

f   m   r   d   t₁   l₁

Will - um   he   had   se - ven   sons,   se - ven   sons,   se - ven   sons,

Will - um   he   had   se - ven sons and   this   is   what they   did.

Activities

The children take it in turns to suggest a mime, e.g. chopping wood, drawing water, milking cows. The song is repeated to accompany the actions.

☆

56

French action song

f m r d t₁ l₁

Lit - tle John - ny dan - ces, On my thumb he dan - ces,

On my thumb, thumb, thumb, John - ny pup - pet dan - ces.

f – m – r – d – t₁ – l₁

2 Little Johnny dances,
On my arm he dances (*repeat*)
On my arm, arm, arm,
** On my thumb, thumb, thumb,
Johnny puppet dances.

** Repeat these two bars as necessary.

(Actions as appropriate.)

3 Little Johnny dances
On my head he dances (*repeat*)
** On my head, . . . arm, . . . thumb, . . .
Johnny puppet dances.

——— Activities ———

Actions

The words of the song suggest appropriate actions. Again, the teacher should encourage even, rhythmic movements.

57

Children's game

| s | f | m | r | d | t₁ | l₁ | s₁ |

Pee, Pee, Pol - ly - an - na, Pee, Pee, Pol - ly - an - na

Pee, Pee, Pol - ly - an - na, ear - ly in the morn - ing.

This is the way the tea - cher stands, Folds her arms, claps her hands.

This is the way the Scots - men dance. Whoops! don't be chee - ky!

Activities

Game

One child skips around inside the moving circle.

On 'This is the way the teacher stands' the children stand still and do the following actions while the child in the middle also does the actions in front of a partner in the ring:
(a) on 'folds her arms' – fold arms;
(b) on 'claps her hands' – clap hands;
(c) on 'this is the way the Scotsmen dance' – attempt Highland fling;
(d) on 'Whoops! don't be cheeky' – turn outwards and flick up imaginary kilts.

The game starts again and progresses as follows: the original child and partner skip around inside the moving circle and the game continues in this way until the circle is dissolved.

58

Traditional rhyme

Ap - ples, peach - es, pears and plums, Tell me when your birth - day comes.

59

Pig - gy on the rail - way, pick - ing up the stones;

Up came an en - gine and broke poor pig - gy's bones.

'Oh!' said Pig - gy. 'That's not fair!'

'Toot!' said the en - gine dri - ver. 'I don't care!'

60

Traditional rhyme

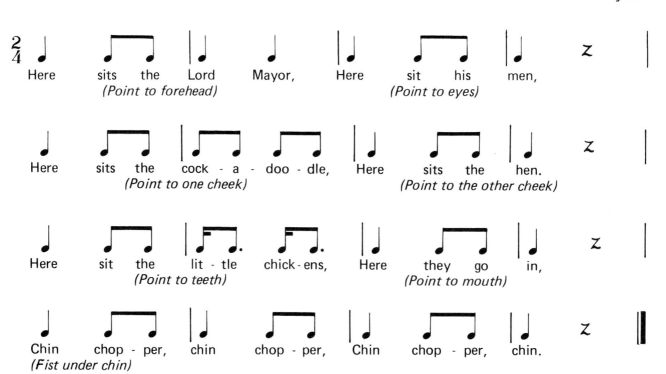

Here sits the Lord Mayor, Here sit his men,
(Point to forehead) *(Point to eyes)*

Here sits the cock-a-doo-dle, Here sits the hen.
(Point to one cheek) *(Point to the other cheek)*

Here sit the lit-tle chick-ens, Here they go in,
(Point to teeth) *(Point to mouth)*

Chin chop-per, chin chop-per, Chin chop-per, chin.
(Fist under chin)

Activities

Actions
The traditional movements for this rhyme
are outlined under the music above.

61

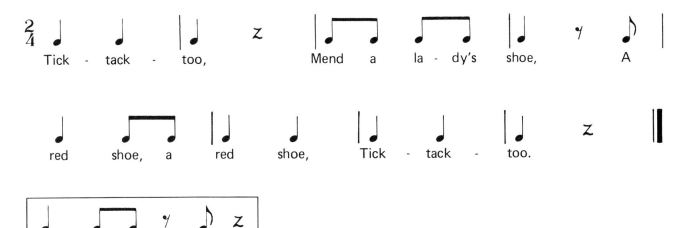

Tick - tack - too, Mend a la - dy's shoe, A red shoe, a red shoe, Tick - tack - too.

2 Tick-tack-too,
Mend a giant's shoe,
A black shoe, a black shoe,
Tick-tack-too.

3 Tick-tack-too,
Mend a baby's shoe,
A white shoe, a white shoe,
Tick-tack-too.

4 Tick-tack-too,
Mend a horse's shoe,
An iron shoe, an iron shoe,
Tick-tack-too.

62

Traditional rhyme

Zin - ty tin - ty tup-pen-ny bun, The cook came out to have some fun. He had some fun, he beat the drum, Zin - ty tin - ty tup-pen-ny bun.

63

An e-le-phant goes like this and that. He's ter-ri-bly big and he's ter-ri-bly fat.

He has no fin-gers, he has no toes, But good-ness gra-cious, what a nose!

Activities

Actions

The children will be able to devise many appropriate actions and movements to this rhyme.

☆

64

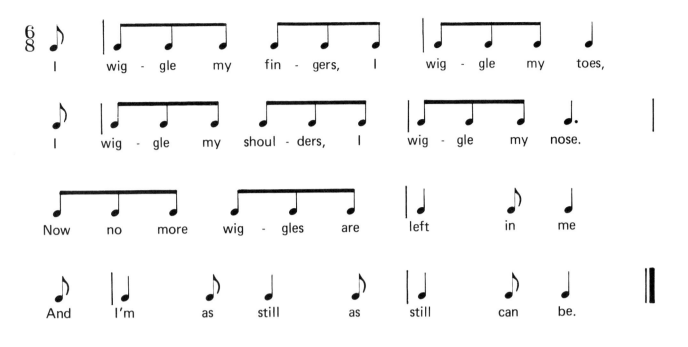

I wig - gle my fin - gers, I wig - gle my toes,

I wig - gle my shoul - ders, I wig - gle my nose.

Now no more wig - gles are left in me

And I'm as still as still can be.

Activities

Actions

It will be useful (and amusing!) for the
children to practise these smaller
movements to this rhyme.

65

s   m

Hey!   Hey!   Look   at   me!   I   am   smil - ing.   Can   you   see?

Activities

Game

A circle is formed with a chosen child in the centre. The child can replace 'smiling' with a descriptive '-ing' word of a selected action, e.g. swaying. The circle steps the pulse as the chosen child sings and performs the actions. The song is then repeated with everyone singing and performing the action.

☆

66

s   m

Traditional children's skipping chant

Ted - dy   Bear,   Ted - dy   Bear   touch   the   ground,

Ted - dy   Bear,   Ted - dy   Bear   turn   right   round.

2 Teddy Bear, Teddy Bear climb the stairs,
Teddy Bear, Teddy Bear say your prayers.

3 Teddy Bear, Teddy Bear switch off the light,
Teddy Bear, Teddy Bear say, 'Goodnight'.

Activities

Actions

The children can make their favourite bear perform the movements, or they themselves can play the part of a teddy bear.

☆

67

s   m

Traditional children's game (England)

LEADER   RESPONSE   LEADER   RESPONSE

Here   I   come.   Where   from?   Lon - don.   What's   your   trade?

LEADER   RESPONSE

Le - mon - ade.   Give   us   some,   don't   be   a - fraid.

s – m

Activities

Game

At the end of the song the Leader chooses someone and pretends to pour him/her a glass of lemonade. This person 'drinks', and then becomes the new Leader.

68

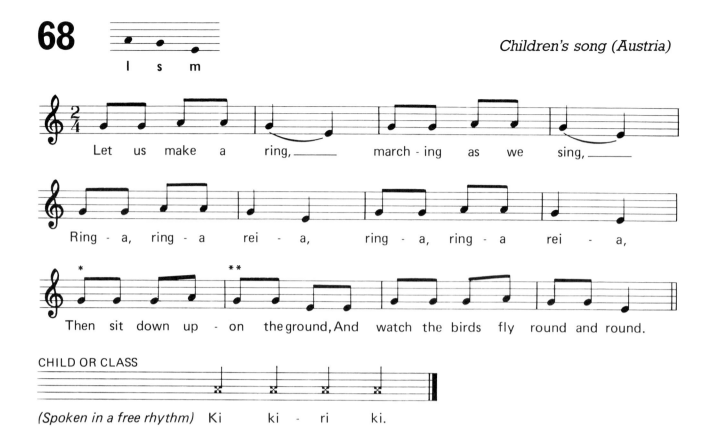

Children's song (Austria)

l   s   m

Let us make a ring, _____ march - ing as we sing, _____

Ring - a, ring - a rei - a, ring - a, ring - a rei - a,

Then sit down up - on the ground, And watch the birds fly round and round.

CHILD OR CLASS

(Spoken in a free rhythm) Ki ki - ri ki.

Activities

Game

The children make a circle and march
round singing. At * they sit down. At **
they flap their arms in imitation of birds'
wings. On the spoken 'Ki kiri ki' they jump
up and resume the march and song.

☆

69

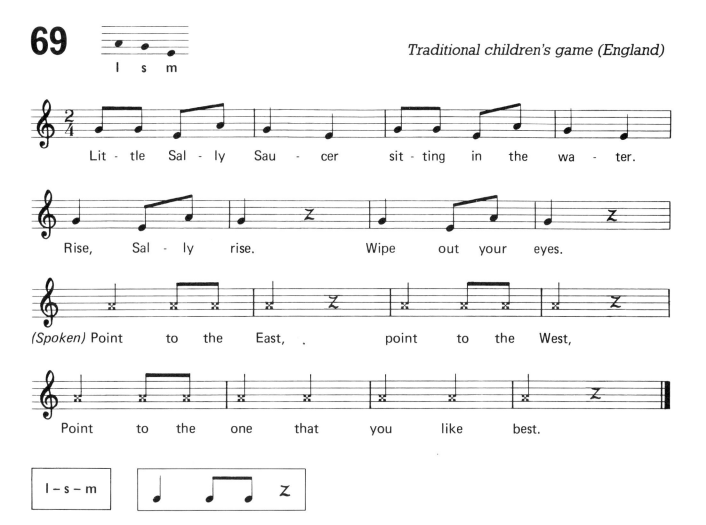

Traditional children's game (England)

Lit - tle Sal - ly Sau - cer sit - ting in the wa - ter.

Rise, Sal - ly rise. Wipe out your eyes.

(Spoken) Point to the East, . point to the West,

Point to the one that you like best.

Activities

Game

The children make a circle with the chosen child in the middle. Everyone sings as the child acts out the words. The spoken section is performed with the child's eyes closed. Whoever is being pointed to at the end will become the next 'Sally'.

Alternatively, all the children may wish to join in performing the spoken actions.

— ☆ —

70

l   s   m

Rat - a - tat - tat!   Who is that?   Ted - dy in his fun - ny hat.

— Activities —

Game

From a box of hats behind a screen, a child selects one to wear. When ready, s/he sings: 'Rat-a-tat-tat'. As the children sing the rest of the song, the child comes from behind the screen in time for the children to complete the song with, e.g. 'Mary in her big black hat'.

☆

71

s   m   d

Tick - tock,   tick - tock,   tell the time true,

Tick - tock,   tick - tock,   half past two.

2 Tick-tock, tick-tock, tell me again,
    Tick-tock, tick-tock, half past ten.

3 Tick-tock, tick-tock, I shall be late,
    Tick-tock, tick-tock, half past eight.

4 (Own verse)

72

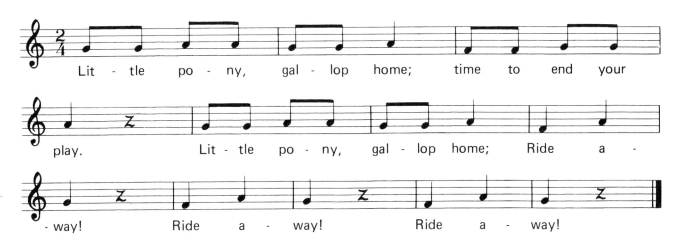

Lit - tle po - ny, gal - lop home; time to end your play. Lit - tle po - ny, gal - lop home; Ride a - way! Ride a - way! Ride a - way!

m – r – d

73

Dutch song

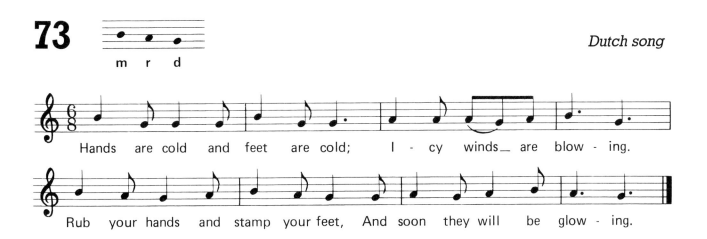

Hands are cold and feet are cold; I - cy winds— are blow - ing. Rub your hands and stamp your feet, And soon they will be glow - ing.

m – r – d

Activities

Actions

The words of the song suggest plenty of appropriate actions and gestures to accompany the singing.

74

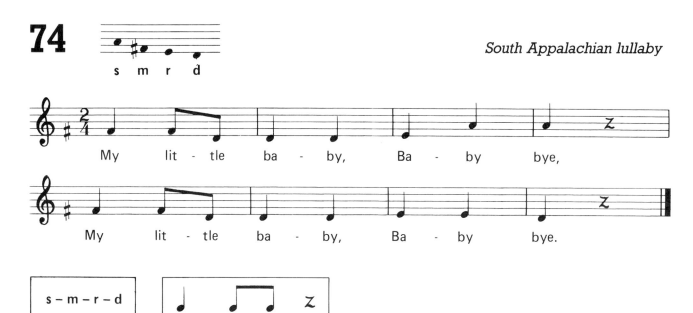

South Appalachian lullaby

My lit - tle ba - by, Ba - by bye,

My lit - tle ba - by, Ba - by bye.

75

German song

Sleep, ba - by, sleep; Fa - ther tends the sheep; Mo - ther shakes the

dream - land tree, And down come all the dreams for thee. Sleep, ba - by, sleep.

76

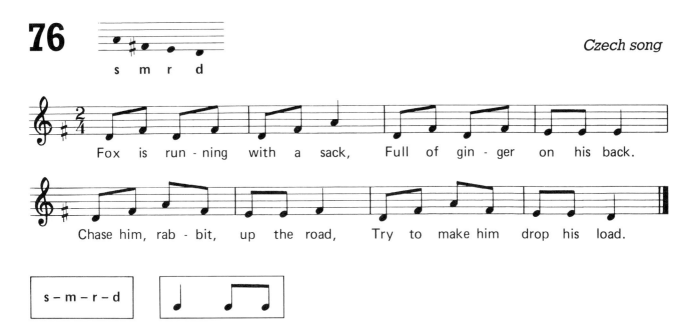

s   m   r   d

Czech song

Fox is run - ning with a sack, Full of gin - ger on his back.

Chase him, rab - bit, up the road, Try to make him drop his load.

Activities

Game

The children sit in a circle facing inwards, the 'fox' sitting next to the 'rabbit'. When the singing starts, the 'fox' stands and, placing a load on his back (e.g. a bean bag or – more difficult – a slippery object), starts to run clockwise outside the circle. On the word 'chase' the 'rabbit' quickly jumps up, following the 'fox' at high speed with the aim of touching the 'fox' before he can return to his place.

☆

77

Traditional folk song (America)

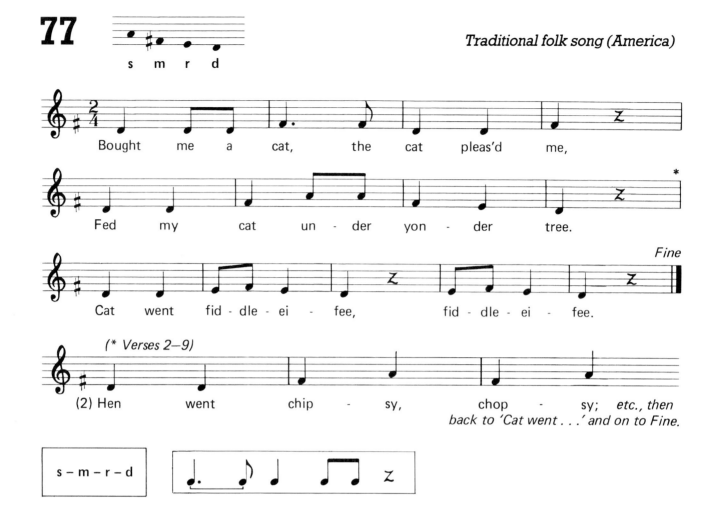

s   m   r   d

Bought me a cat, the cat pleas'd me,

Fed my cat un - der yon - der tree.

Fine

Cat went fid - dle - ei - fee, fid - dle - ei - fee.

(* Verses 2—9)

(2) Hen went chip - sy, chop - sy; *etc., then back to 'Cat went . . .' and on to Fine.*

s – m – r – d

2   Bought me a hen . . . . . . went chipsy, chopsy;
3   Bought me a duck . . . . . . went slishy, sloshy;
4   Bought me a sheep . . . . . . went baa, baa;
5   Bought me a horse . . . . . . went neigh, neigh;
6   Bought me a goose . . . . . . went qua! qua!
7   Bought me a cow . . . . . . went moo, moo;
8   Bought me a baby . . . . . . went mummy, mummy;
9   Bought me a woman . . . . . . went darling, darling.

This is a cumulative song in which words of the
preceding verses are repeated in the way shown
for verse 2, and always working back to 'cat
went fiddle-ei-fee'.

78

Ham - mer - ing here, ham - mer - ing there, Ham - mer - ing nails,

mak - ing a chair. Ham - mer - ing straight, ham - mer - ing true,

Hit ev - 'ry nail as the car - pen - ters do. *(Spoken)* Whack! Whack!

Traditional singing rhyme

I'm a lit - tle Dutch - girl, Dutch - girl, Dutch - girl.

I'm a lit - tle Dutch - girl, far, far a - way.

Boys: I'm a little Dutchboy, Dutchboy, Dutchboy
I'm a little Dutchboy, far, far away.

Girls: Go away! I hate you, hate you, hate you;
Go away! I hate you, far, far away.

Boys: Why do you hate me, hate me, hate me?
Why do you hate me, far, far away?

Girls: Because you stole my necklace, necklace, necklace,
Because you stole my necklace, far, far away.

Boys: Here is your necklace, necklace, necklace,
Here is your necklace, far, far away.

Everyone: Now we're getting married, married, married,
Now we're getting married, far, far away.

Everyone: Now we're having babies, babies, babies,
Now we're having babies, far, far away.

Everyone: Now we're getting older, older, older,
Now we're getting older, far, far away.

Everyone: Now we're dead forever, ever, ever,
Now we're dead forever, far, far away.

Everyone: Now we're little ghosties, ghosties, ghosties,
Now we're little ghosties, far, far away.

Everyone: Now we're dancing skeletons, skeletons, skeletons,
Now we're dancing skeletons, far, far away.

Activities

Game

The children form up in two lines, facing each other. The 'Dutchgirls' skip towards their partners and retire, perhaps having both hands on their hips. The 'Dutchboys' do likewise in the second verse, sometimes doing a Scottish dance step, with one hand on hip and the other above the head.

When the girls sing 'Go away! I hate you', they turn their backs and stamp their feet. The boys make their peace, pretending to hold out a necklace. When they announce they are to be married they link elbows and dance round, or cross arms and twirl. Thereafter, the actions are as the words of the verses suggest.

80

Traditional rhyme

l s m r d

Star - light, star bright, first star I've seen to - night.

Wish I may, wish I might have the wish I wish to - night.

l – s – m – r – d

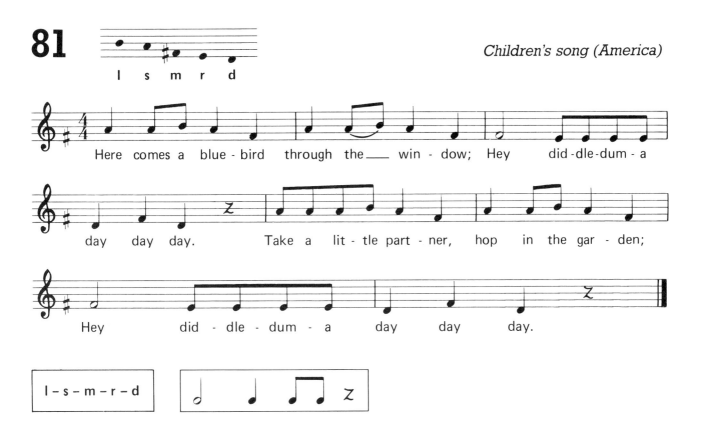

81

Children's song (America)

l s m r d

Here comes a blue - bird through the ___ win - dow; Hey did -dle-dum - a

day day day. Take a lit - tle part - ner, hop in the gar - den;

Hey did - dle - dum - a day day day.

l – s – m – r – d

Activities

Game

The children stand in a circle with hands joined. One child (the 'bird') walks round, outside the circle, until (on the word 'window') s/he enters the circle by passing through arched arms. On 'Take a little partner' this child takes a partner from the circle and, with both hands joined, they face each other and gallop out through the opening (from which the partner was taken) – and back again. The first child then joins the circle and the partner becomes the 'bird'.

82   *Game song (America)*

l s m r d

But - ton you must wan - der, wan - der, wan - der.

But - ton you must wan - der ev - 'ry - where.

Bright eyes will find you, sharp eyes will find you,

But - ton you must wan - der ev - 'ry - where.

l – s – m – r – d

Activities

Game

A child is selected to stand in the centre of a circle of children. The children forming the circle have outstretched hands through which is passed a continuous thread or string. A button threaded on the string is transferred secretively from one hand to another round the circle during the singing of the song. The centre child must try to detect who has the button at the end of the song.

☆

2 See the Indian squaws, grinding yellow corn;
  Hiya, hiya, etc . . .

3 See the Indian boys, paddling their canoes;
  Hiya, hiya, etc . . .

4 See the Indian girls, making bowls of clay;
  Hiya, hiya, etc . . .

5 See the Indian braves dance around the fire;
  Hiya, hiya, etc . . .

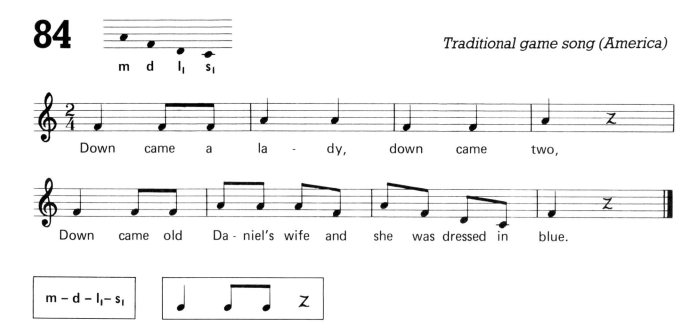

84   m   d   l₁   s₁   *Traditional game song (America)*

Down came a la - dy, down came two,

Down came old Da - niel's wife and she was dressed in blue.

m – d – l₁ – s₁

Activities

Game

Make a circle. Select one child to stand in the middle. The other children walk in a circle and stop just before the word 'blue', as the child in the middle points to one of the circle-children and sings the name of the colour s/he is wearing. This second child goes to the outside of the circle and, as the game continues, walks in the opposite direction to the circle. The game ends when all the circle-children are in the outer circle.

(It is usual for the child in the centre to choose a child in blue initially, so that the rhyme works – at least for the first verse.)

85

f m r d

Traditional children's game (Britain)

Sal - ly go round the sun, Sal - ly go round the moon,

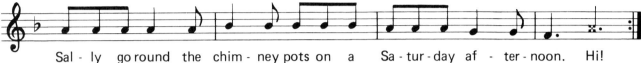

Sal - ly go round the chim - ney pots on a Sa - tur - day af - ter - noon. Hi!

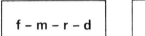

Activities

Game

A small group of six or seven children join hands and whirl around in a circle at quite a fast pace. After the final word, they kick their legs into the air and shout. The song is repeated without a pause. The direction of the turning circle can be varied.

86

Folk song (America)

s f m r d

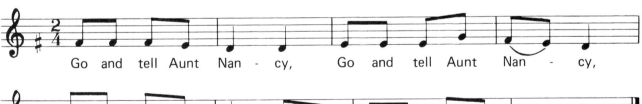

Go and tell Aunt Nan - cy, Go and tell Aunt Nan - cy,

Go and tell Aunt Nan - cy The old grey goose is dead.

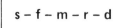

2 The one that she'd been saving, (*three times*)
To make her feather bed.

4 She left nine goslings, (*three times*)
To scratch for their own bread.

3 She died last Friday, (*three times*)
Standing on her head.

Traditional children's game (Britain)

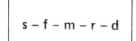

Verses: (Using the same tune.)

1 First the farmer sows his seed,
Then he stands and takes his ease,
Stamps his feet and claps his hands,
And turns around to view the land.

Chorus: Oats and beans . . .

2 Waiting for a partner,
Waiting for a partner,
Open the ring and take one in,
And kiss her in the centre.

Chorus: Oats and beans . . .

3 Now you're married you must obey,
You must be true in all you say,
You must be kind, you must be good,
And help your wife to chop the wood.

Chorus: Oats and beans . . .

Activities

Game
The children form a circle with the 'farmer' in the centre.
Chorus: All dance round the 'farmer' skipping in the middle.
Verse 1: The circle stops, and everyone performs the actions with the
'farmer'.
Chorus: As before.
Verse 2: The circle stops, and the 'farmer' chooses a partner.
Chorus: 'Farmer' and 'wife' dance together, while others dance round.
Verse 3: The circle stops, and the children wag their fingers at
'farmer' and 'wife' as they sing.
Chorus: As before.

88

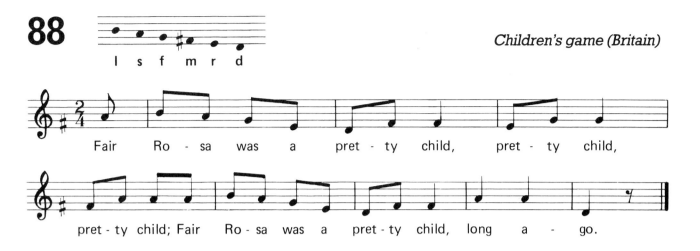

Children's game (Britain)

Fair Ro - sa was a pret - ty child, pret - ty child,

pret - ty child; Fair Ro - sa was a pret - ty child, long a - go.

2 And she lived in a big high tower, . . . long ago.

3 A wicked fairy cast a spell, . . . long ago.

4 Fair Rosa slept for a hundred years, . . . long ago.

5 A great big forest grew around, . . . long ago.

6 A handsome prince came riding by, . . . long ago.

7 He took his sword and cut it down, . . . long ago.

8 He kissed Fair Rosa's lily-white hand, . . . long ago.

9 And ev'rybody's happy now, . . . long ago.

Activities

Game

The children circle around 'Fair Rosa' who stands in the middle. The 'handsome prince' stands outside the circle and the 'wicked fairy' is inside.

On the second verse the children stand still and raise their arms, still holding hands, to make a tower formation.

Then the 'wicked fairy' moves around 'Fair Rosa', waving her arms and casting an imaginary spell. The children in the circle do the same.

On the fourth verse 'Fair Rosa' falls down and pretends to sleep, while the circle moves in closer to the sleeping child, the children making their arms form branches by raising them above 'Fair Rosa'.

The 'handsome prince' gallops around the circle on an imaginary horse, then he goes round cutting the branches away.

The circle falls back from the sleeping 'princess' and the 'prince' wakes her up by taking her hand.

These two now join hands and twirl around while the other children clap hands.

These three characters now choose three new children to play the game again.

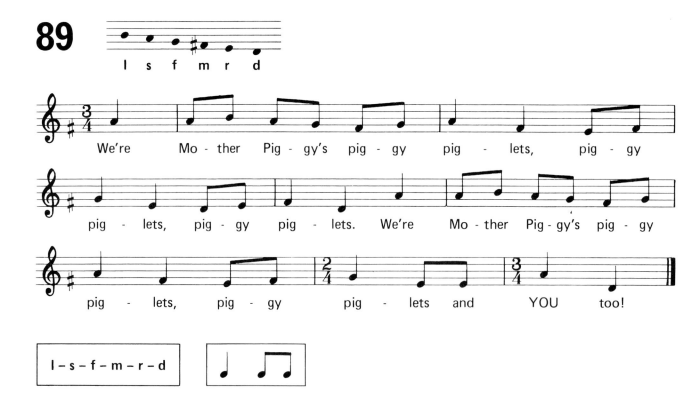

89

l s f m r d

We're Mo - ther Pig - gy's pig - gy pig - lets, pig - gy pig - lets, pig - gy pig - lets. We're Mo - ther Pig - gy's pig - gy pig - lets, pig - gy pig - lets and YOU too!

l – s – f – m – r – d

Activities

Game

The children stand in a circle with an arm-length space between each child. A chosen child weaves in and out between the children as s/he goes round the circle. On the word 'you', s/he faces and points to the child arrived at. The song is sung again as the second child leads the first child round the circle in a similar way. The 'litter of piglets' is added to, until the circle is dissolved. The game could be played with two or three 'litters' moving round one circle.

☆

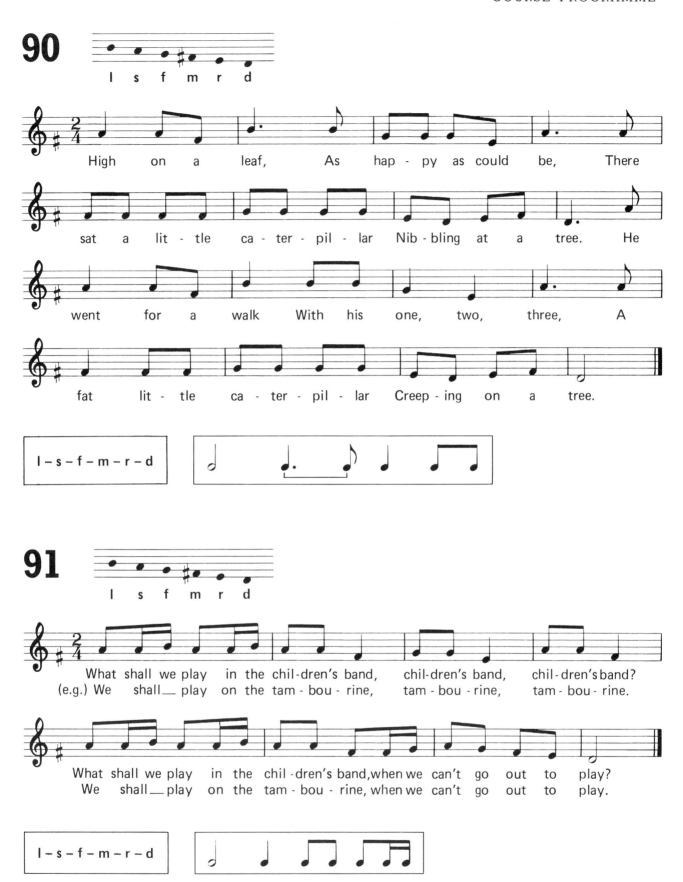

90

l s f m r d

High on a leaf, As hap - py as could be, There sat a lit - tle ca - ter - pil - lar Nib - bling at a tree. He went for a walk With his one, two, three, A fat lit - tle ca - ter - pil - lar Creep - ing on a tree.

l – s – f – m – r – d

91

l s f m r d

What shall we play in the chil - dren's band, chil - dren's band, chil - dren's band?
(e.g.) We shall__ play on the tam - bou - rine, tam - bou - rine, tam - bou - rine.

What shall we play in the chil - dren's band, when we can't go out to play?
We shall__ play on the tam - bou - rine, when we can't go out to play.

l – s – f – m – r – d

Any available and suitable instruments can be played to the pulse, or the children can 'play' imaginary instruments with mimed actions, also to the pulse. Alternatively, have a group of children perform a rhythm ostinato to accompany the song, e.g.

92

A Jewish song for the Festival of Lights (Hanukkah)

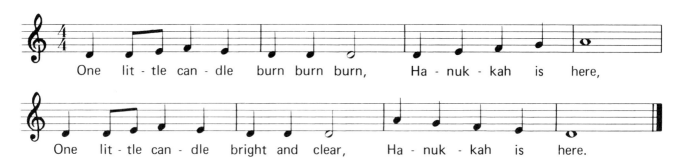

One lit - tle can - dle burn burn burn, Ha - nuk - kah is here,

One lit - tle can - dle bright and clear, Ha - nuk - kah is here.

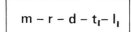 

2 Two little candles . . .

3 Three little candles . . .

(. . . and so on, up to 'Eight . . .')

93

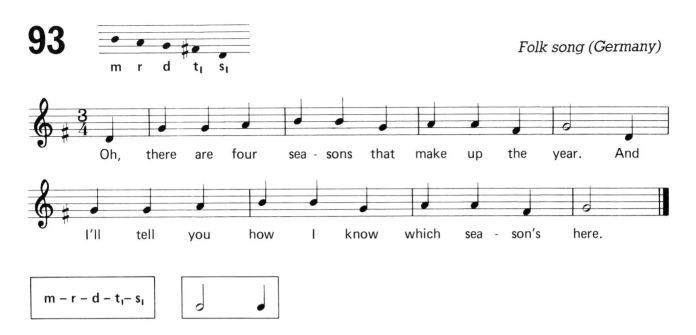

Folk song (Germany)

Oh, there are four sea-sons that make up the year. And I'll tell you how I know which sea-son's here.

2 The springtime brings flowers; the summer brings sun;
The autumn brings harvests and cool mists will come.

3 The season of winter brings ice and brings snow;
My hands will be frozen when cold winds do blow.

94

Far - mer Higgs, Far - mer Higgs, Far - mer Higgs has three black pigs, three black pigs, three black pigs.

2 Farmer Howes has two brown cows.

3 Farmer Penn has just one hen.

4 Farmer Hall has nothing at all.

95

Traditional children's action song

m r d t₁ l₁ s₁

A - lice the ca - mel has two humps,
(one/no)

A - lice the ca - mel has two humps,
(one/no)

Last time go to ⊕

A - lice the ca - mel has two humps, so
(one/no)

Repeat for 'one' and 'no humps'

go A - lice go. Boom, boom, boom.

⊕

A - lice is a horse! Boom, boom, boom, boom.

$m - r - d - t_1 - l_1 - s_1$

Activities

Game

The children form a circle with arms interlocked across the shoulders. The circle turns as the song is sung.
However, on each 'two (one/no) humps' all dip the body from the knees, and up again.
On each 'boom' all hips sway vigorously.

☆

96   *Traditional singing game*

Have you seen the muf - fin man, the muf - fin man, the muf - fin man?

Have you seen the muf - fin man who comes from down your way?

| m – r – d – t₁– l₁– s₁ | |

2   Yes, I've seen the muffin man, the muffin man, the muffin man.
     Yes, I've seen the muffin man who comes from down our way.

Activities

Game

The children form a circle. A child in the centre is blindfolded and holds a long stick. At the end of the songs s/he touches, or points to someone in the circle who then grasps the other end of the stick. The centre child has three questions s/he may ask requiring 'yes' or 'no' answers, during which s/he must guess the name of the child at the other end. If s/he guesses correctly they change places.

97

f m r d t₁ l₁ s₁

I walked to the top of the hill, I walked to the top of the hill. It be-gan to rain, So I came down a-gain, And I think it's rain-ing still.

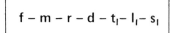

2 I ran to the grocer's shop,
I ran to the grocer's shop,
But the shop was full
So I went to school
Without my lollipop.

3 I went to fly my plane,
I went to fly my plane.
It flew up in the air
But I don't know where
'Cos it never came back again.

Song collection (rhythm-solfa notation)

1 Hello, how are you?

9 I, I, me oh my!

10 See-saw

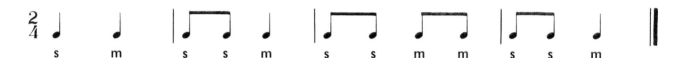

11 Cuckoo! Cherry tree

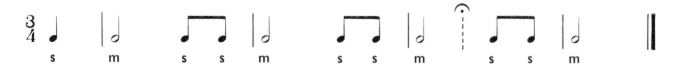

12 Pears for pies

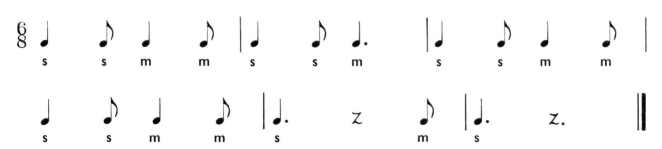

13 Rap-a tap-a

14 Snail, snail

15 Rain, rain, go away!

16 Round and round

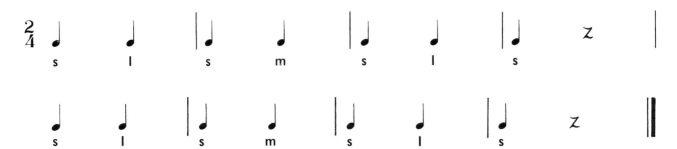

17 Tap, tap, tap!

(Whisper the rhythm as above for the remaining words.)

18 What shall we do?

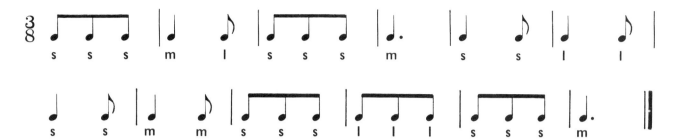

19 Roll up! Here's the fair

20 Rain on the green grass

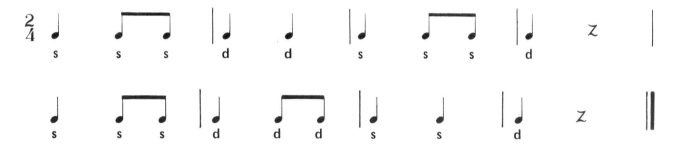

21 I see you

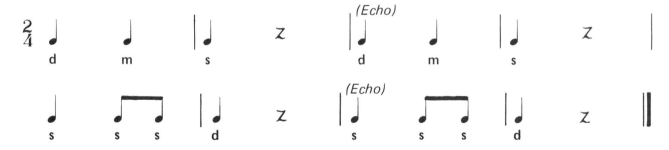

22 Bells in the steeple

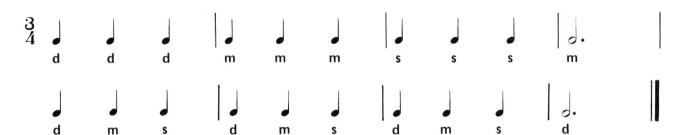

23 Jack-in-the-box

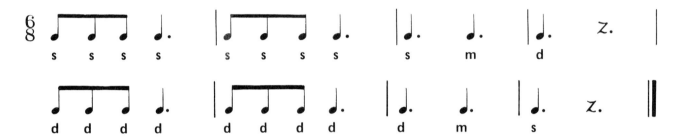

24 Can you tap your fingers?

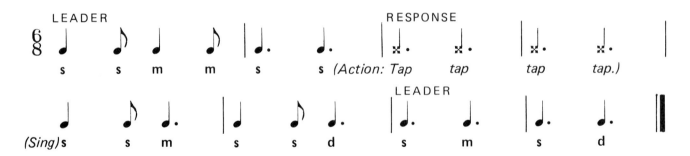

25 Tick-tock, tick-tock, see my clock

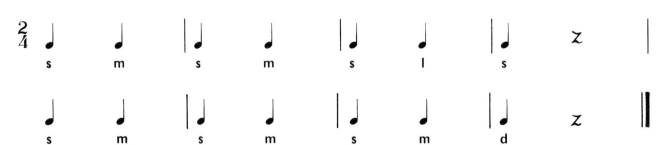

26 This is how a drummer-boy/girl

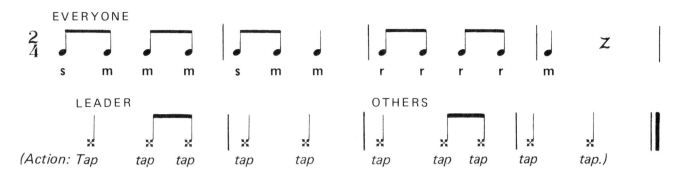

27 Rabbit in the hollow

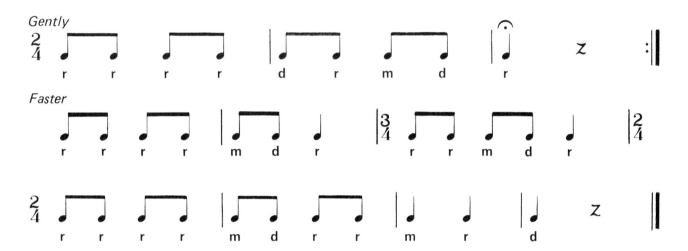

28 Here we go

29 Make the porridge in a pan

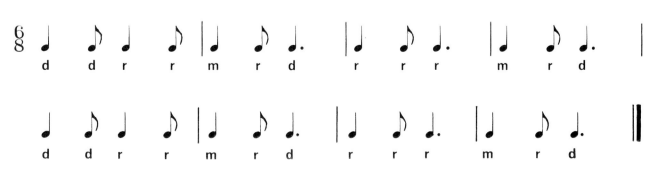

30 Listen, listen, here I come

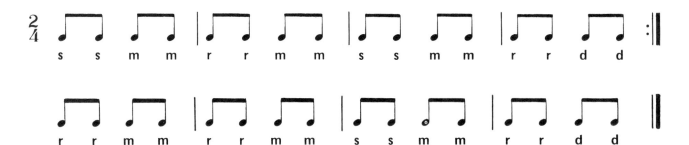

31 Little Arabella Miller

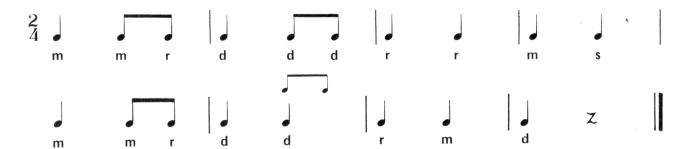

32 I have a dog

33 Lots of rosy apples

34 Who is that I see?

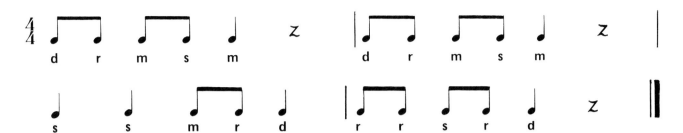

35 Engine, engine

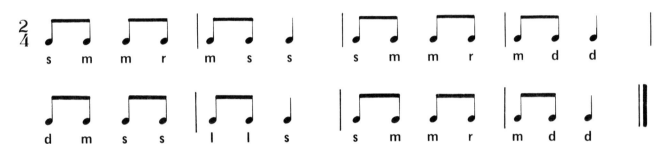

36 Tom cats, alley cats

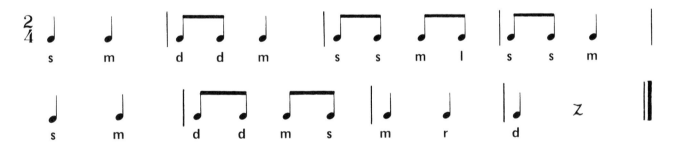

37 Who has the penny?

Examples:

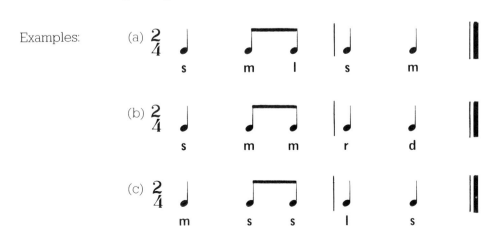

38 Here is the beehive

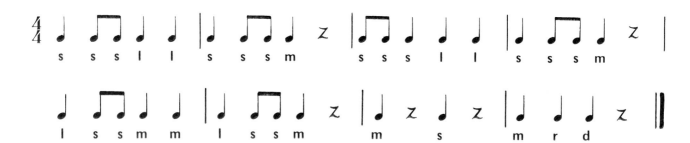

39 Bow, wow, wow!

40 Snowman, snowman

41 A goblin lives in our house

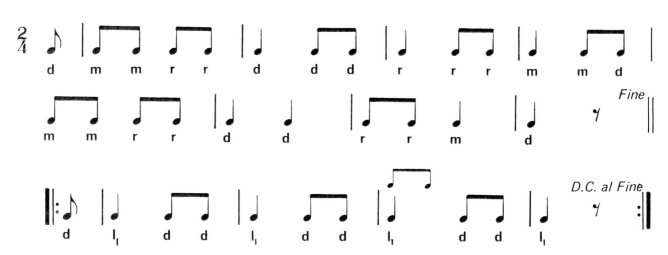

42 Chuffa, chuffa, chuff!

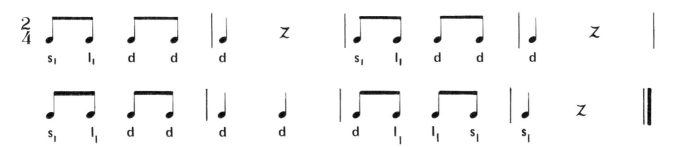

43 Hickety tickety

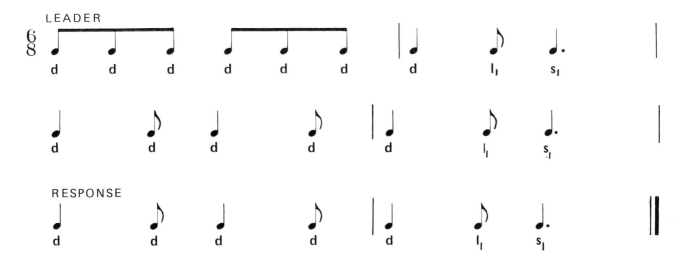

44 See my wellingtons

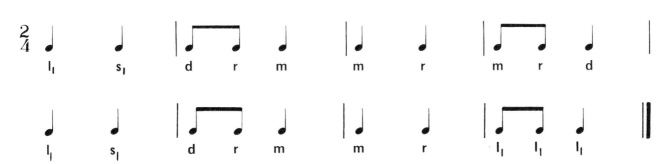

45 Ding, dong

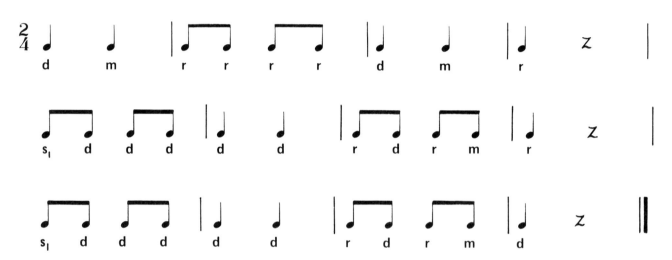

46 Tell me, shepherdess

47 Pease pudding hot

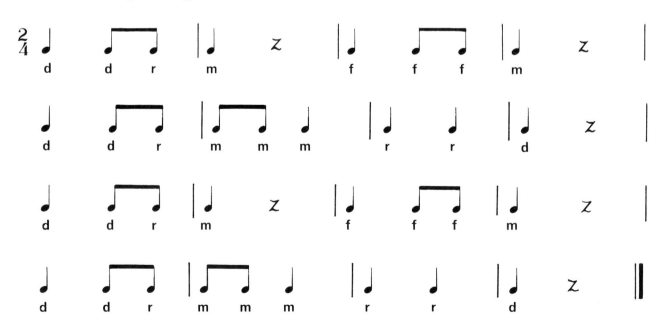

48 Down the hill

49 Pitter patter

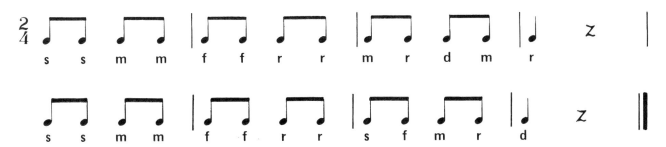

50 Clip, clop

51 Once a man fell in a well

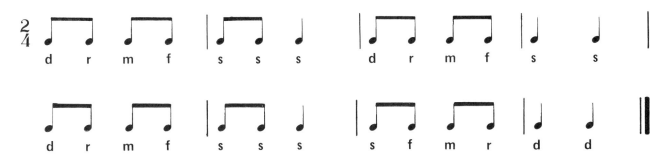

52 Hush, my dear

TEACHER
Gently lilting

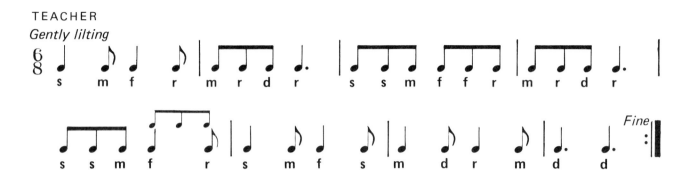

CHILDREN
Very fast

53 Glowing candle-light

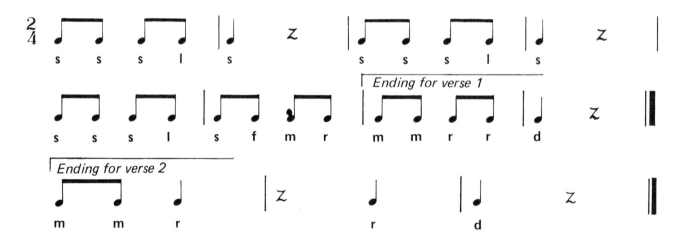

54 Pancake Tuesday

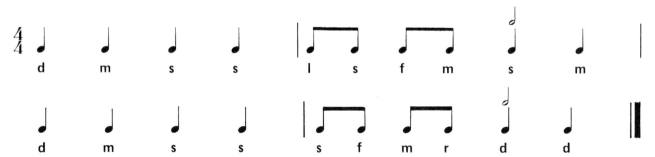

55 Willum he had seven sons

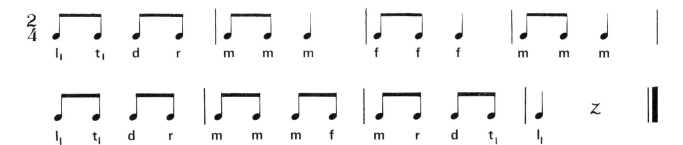

56 Little Johnny dances

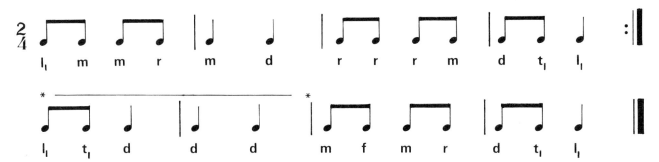

57 Pee, Pee, Pollyanna

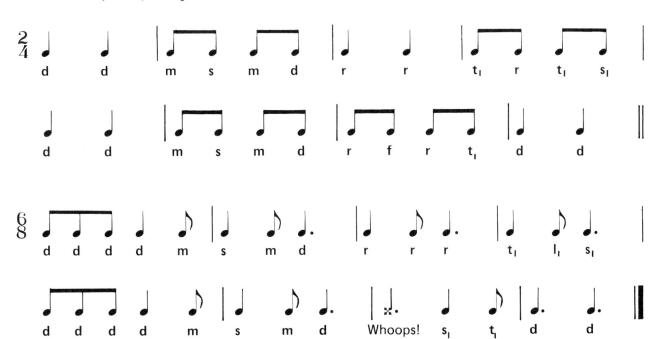

Note: The following songs provide supplementary material to the 'core'
songs **1–57**.
See note on page 61, and reference on pages 11–12.

65 Hey! Hey! Look at me!

66 Teddy Bear, Teddy Bear

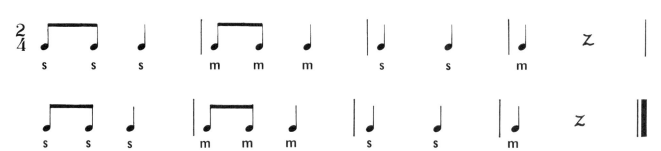

67 Here I come

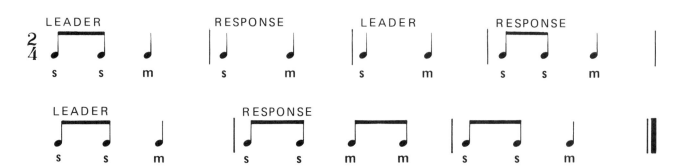

68 Let us make a ring

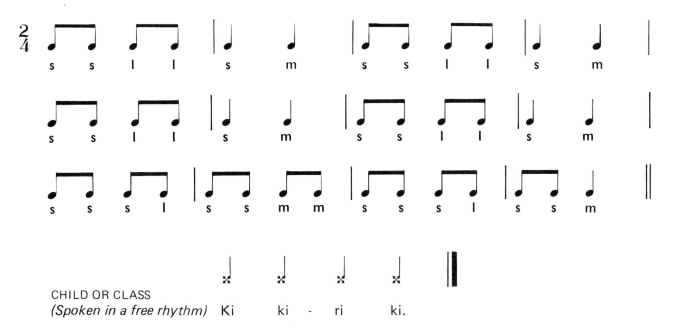

CHILD OR CLASS
(Spoken in a free rhythm) Ki ki - ri ki.

69 Little Sally Saucer

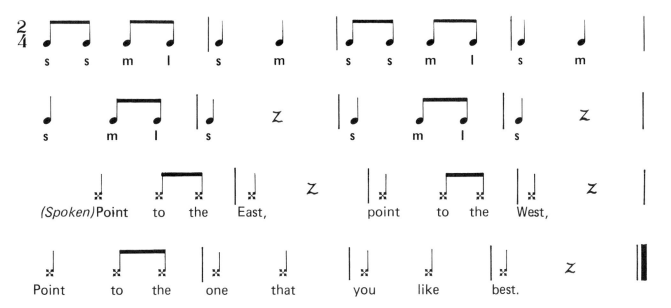

(Spoken) Point to the East, point to the West,

Point to the one that you like best.

70 Rat-a-tat-tat!

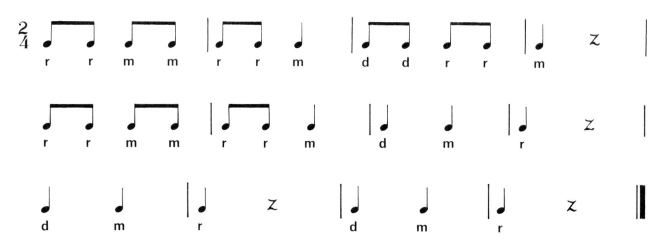

m m m s   m m s   m m s s   l s m

71 Tick-tock, tick-tock, tell the time

s m   s m   d d m   s

s m   s m   s m   d

72 Little pony, gallop home

r r m m   r r m   d d r r   m

r r m m   r r m   d m   r

d m   r   d m   r

73 Hands are cold

m d d   d m d d   r r r d r   m   d

m r d r   m r d   d r d r   m r   d

74 My little baby

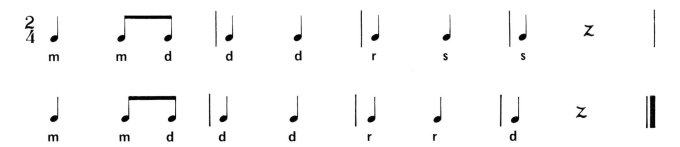

75 Sleep, baby, sleep

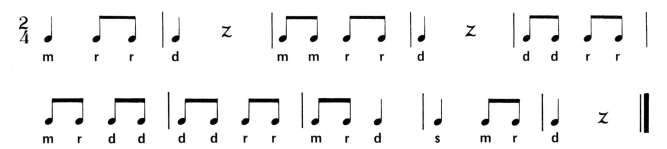

76 Fox is running

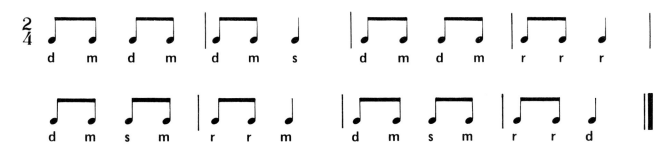

77 Bought me a cat

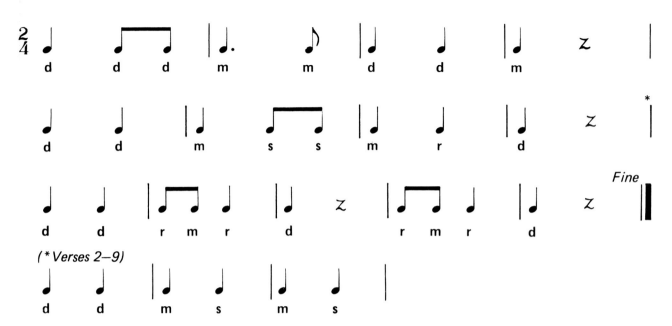

(*Verses 2–9)

78 Hammering here

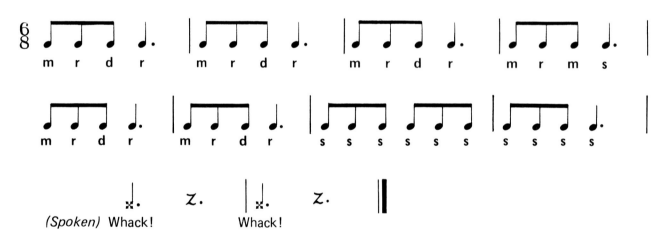

(Spoken) Whack!   Whack!

79 I'm a little Dutch-girl

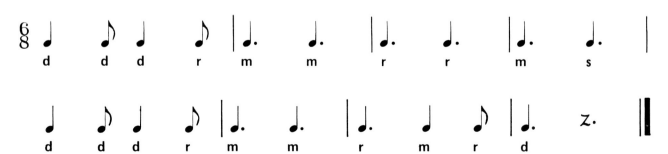

80 Starlight, star bright

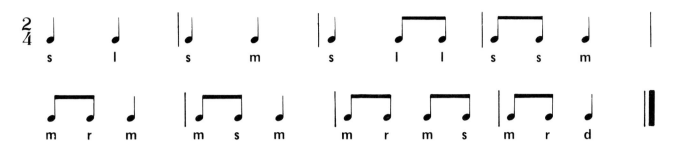

81 Here comes a bluebird

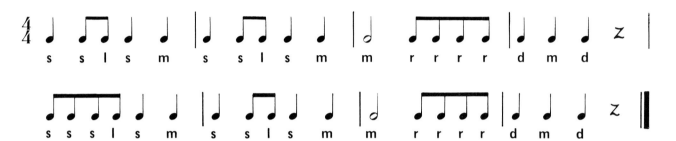

82 Button you must wander

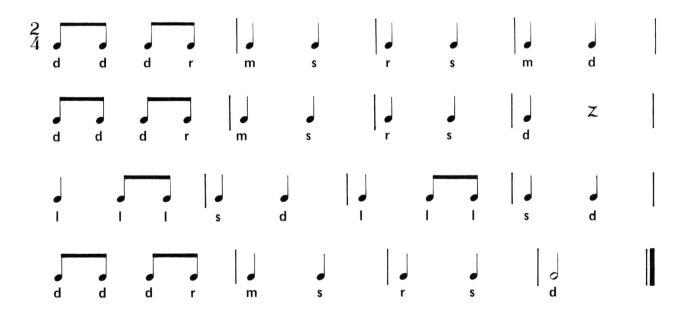

83 See the Indian chief

$\frac{2}{4}$ m d d d d 𝄽 | m d d d d 𝄽 |

d l̦ l̦ l̦ | d l̦ l̦ l̦ | d l̦ l̦ ș | l̦ 𝄽 ‖

84 Down came a lady

$\frac{2}{4}$ d d d m | m d | d m | 𝄽 |

d d d m | m m d | m d l̦ ș | d 𝄽 ‖

85 Sally go round the sun

$\frac{6}{8}$ d d d d d d | 𝄽. | r r r r r r | 𝄽. |

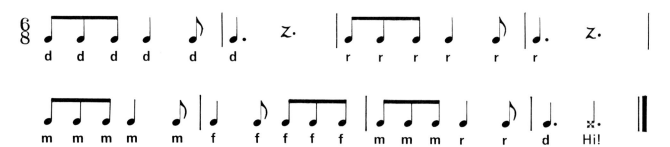

m m m m m f | f f f f | m m m r | r d Hi! ‖

86 Go and tell Aunt Nancy

$\frac{2}{4}$ m m m r | d d | r r r f | m r d |

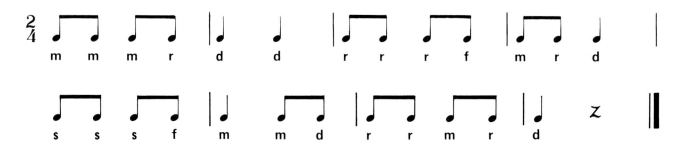

s s s f | m m d | r r m r | d 𝄽 ‖

87 Oats and beans

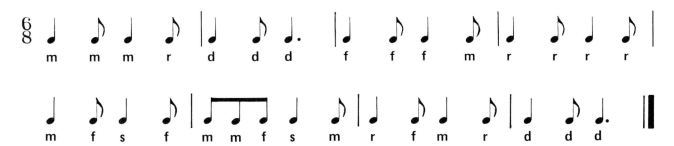

88 Fair Rosa was a pretty child

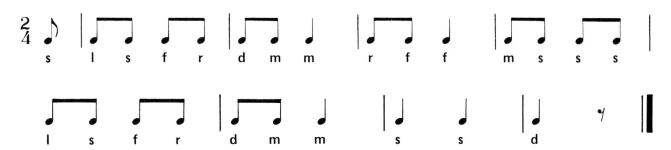

89 We're Mother Piggy's piggy piglets

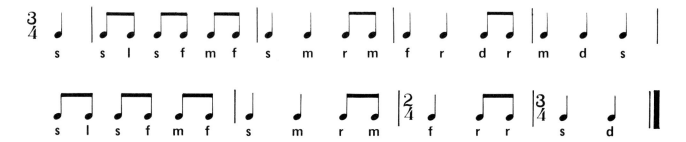

90 High on a leaf

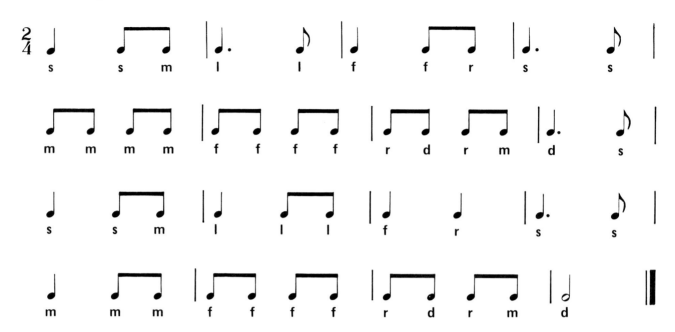

91 What shall we play?

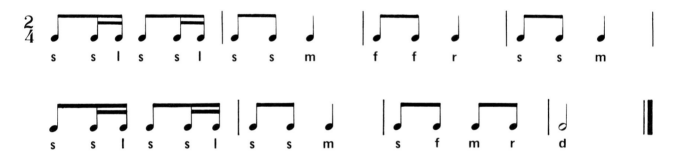

92 One little candle

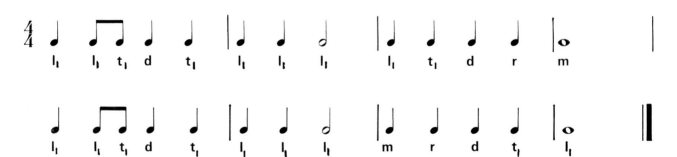

93 Oh, there are four seasons

94 Farmer Higgs

95 Alice the camel

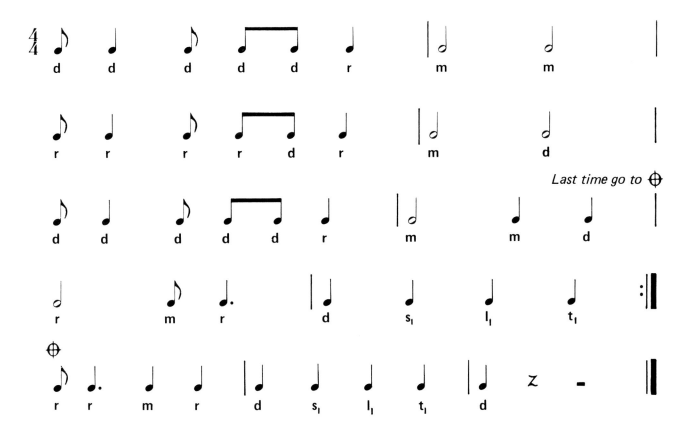

96 Have you seen the muffin man?

97 I walked to the top of the hill

Guidance for teachers

- This section sets out the underlying principles and aims of **Growing with Music: Key Stage 1**. In addition, it contains useful information and explanation concerning the practical applications of the *Course programme*. Familiarity with *Guidance for teachers* is essential for an accurate interpretation and implementation of the principles, aims and contents of **Growing with Music: Key Stage 1**.

Musical thinking and the inner ear

Children acquire music as they acquire language – by listening, imitating and by using it for their own purposes. For this to happen a process of *musical thinking* must take place, a process of inner hearing made possible by the facility of short- and long-term memories – the ability to 'audiate', in fact.

By using the voice as the performing medium ('performing' in the sense of participating), each child is encouraged *to make his/her own musical sound.* This demands that the child hears *internally* not only what has been performed (using memory) but also what is to be performed (using memory and improvising).

This course stimulates the development of the inner ear and musical thinking by asking children to:

a imitate sung phrases from unknown songs and teacher improvising (short-term memory);

b recall known melodic phrases and sing them either as individuals or as a class (long-term memory);

c sing in their heads known song phrases (memory and thinking voice);

d improvise melodic or rhythmic phrases (memory and thinking voice);

e retain and recall improvised phrases for writing in music notation (memory and thinking voice).

In this way, the children make music their own, as a living language – becoming familiar with the medium and learning to control it with confidence. Eventually, with the gradual introduction of a music notation which has use and meaning because the child knows the sound internally, a process of musical thinking is brought about which the children are able to share with each other and develop for themselves. In fact, it becomes a basis for true musical independence; the 'thinking voice' (see page 155) comes into its own; an education *in* music (not *about* music) is taking place.

Singing

Why singing?

Each child has a voice with several characteristics – the talking voice, shouting voice, whispering voice, singing voice, humming voice and (in a special way) the thinking voice. Each child has a right to discover all these voices and to be given the chance of being skilled in their use.

The singing voice is a fine and free instrument, possessed by each child, with direct access to intellect as well as emotions.

Stages of discovery

There are several learning stages in a child's growing awareness of his/her singing voice. For example, children who are two or three years old might sing in a way which only remotely resembles the contour of a simple melody, taking on more accuracy at a later stage – even though it might not yet match the pitch at which the melody is being sung by the teacher. A more advanced stage is reached when the voice can produce an accurate account of a more complex melody.

Some children will have reached these more advanced learning stages by the age of four; often, however, this is not so. Therefore, it is vital that children receive continuous help and singing opportunities so that their awareness is developed. The encouragement of careful listening and singing, and the use of appropriate repertoire are essential at all stages of vocal development.

A child with an undiscovered voice is a deprived child, restricted in his/her music-making and destined to feel musically and educationally demoralised.

Our voices

Encourage children to be aware of the various types of sound that each voice can produce. Discover with the children:

The Talking Voice;
The Whispering Voice;
The Shouting Voice;
The Humming Voice;
The Singing Voice;
The Thinking Voice.

Practise using these voices. For example:

1 Teacher (whispering): 'Have you brought your whispering voice?' Child (or children), whispering, replies: 'Yes, I have. Yes, I have.'

2 Play 'Who has the penny?' (*Song collection* 37), varying the voices used. Also, play this game so that the responding voice is required to be different from the leading voice.

In this way children become able to distinguish between a voice that is a singing voice and one that is not – an essential stage of understanding for children who experience difficulties in finding their singing voice. All voices are acceptable and usable in the early stages, but we are concerned primarily in helping children to find and develop their singing voice.

The **thinking voice** is in use when the child hears the music 'in his/her head', without making any sound with voice or instrument. A growing use of the thinking voice is essential to the musical development of each child because it encourages the ability to:

a 'internalise' music;
b memorise;
c think in a music dimension.

Some important teaching points

1 Most song learning can be carried out efficiently through imitative response. The children repeat the melodic phrase sung by the teacher.

2 In addition to class/group repetition, the teacher needs to encourage a good deal of individual response because:

a it is a useful way of assessing individual achievement;
b children are usually curious to hear another child sing and can learn from the experience;
c to sing individually is the only way in which a child becomes aware of the sound of his/her singing voice;
d an opportunity is thus created for a positive, supportive and appreciative response by the teacher and the rest of the class;
e in this way, the child grows in confidence;
f the class does not become totally dependent upon the singing of the teacher.

Difficulty in finding the singing voice

Children who have difficulty in establishing their singing voice, or who have difficulty singing **in tune**, may do so for a number of reasons. In some cases, there may be hearing or social problems, but usually the problem can be cured on a one-to-one basis.

The general rule is to begin with what the voice is already doing. For example, if the child is normally singing on one note only (**monotone**) then the starting point for the teacher should be to do the same. The child probably needs to hear his sound reflected back several times. As confidence is established, the teacher moves the last sound of the melodic phrase down one or two steps in pitch, encouraging the pupil to imitate. Later the teacher should try the same procedure but with a starting sound one tone higher or lower. Gradually, the range of sounds and pitch should be widened. Always work in short melodic phrases of great simplicity until, with growing skill and confidence, the child is ready for slightly more complex phrases. Improvised words and melodies are usually best since they can be tailored to individual requirements.

Humming concentrates the pitch activity in the resonating cavities of the head. Head resonances make the notes of higher pitch easier to produce. This and the quiet sound of humming help the child to focus aurally on the sound being made. Encourage the child to produce humming sounds that rise and fall in pitch, suggesting perhaps a car moving away or the sound of an unhappy ghost!

Flowing physical movements are of considerable help to children who experience difficulties. Nervous tension and taut muscles are barriers to solving vocal and aural problems. Find activities in which the child sings and moves with ease – action songs and singing games are especially useful in this respect.

It is important for the teacher to convey a cheerful expectation that the singing voice will be discovered.

The singing sound

The *Song collection* offers material appropriate to children in the early stages of vocal development.

Why improve the singing sound?

1 Every child has a singing voice with potential.

2 In later stages of educational growth children do become aware of those areas of experience which have lacked development. Therefore, if the singing voice is not to remain largely immature, a constant feature of the teaching should be the improvement of the singing voice – its quality and agility.

3 A capable and attractive singing voice is a lifelong possession.

4 Improvement in the singing sound will result from the child's careful listening and imitative response. A developing perception and awareness of the nuances of the singing sound will further the child's general aural abilities.

5 The experience of singing within a body of improved and capable voices makes a unique and indelible impression which, over a period of time, increases the expectation of each child and consequently raises his/her musical standards.

6 It is most important that we provide children with a framework of opportunities to improve the vocal sound according to the age and stage of singing development.

Improvement to the vocal sound can begin once the child has discovered his/her singing voice and is using it with confidence and accuracy. This would normally begin to take place during the third year of this course i.e. the top infant year.

Listening

Only the voice can be a model for the voice. It is never too soon for young children to listen regularly to good models of vocal quality. The children require to know what is considered a better sound and what it is they are trying to achieve. The models must be suitable and should come from various sources; for example, the teacher, another child, a children's choir (live or recorded).

The physical and mental framework

Exploring the singing voice and encouraging good singing habits in young children should always be an enjoyable experience, free from physical and mental tensions. The teacher should see the development of the voice as a continuous and long-term process requiring regular, purposeful and rewarding practice.

When the teacher feels the class is ready to work at improving the singing sound s/he should arrange the children into a convenient, but well-defined standing or sitting group in which optimum eye contact is possible. So arranged, each child is thus encouraged to be aurally alert and receptive and the voice is supported by a suitable breathing posture.

Singing technique

The teacher needs to be aware of certain basic features in singing, and gradually and sensitively encourage children to think about the way in which they sing.

Breathing. A developing awareness and ability in the area of breath control is fundamental to vocal progress. A positive mental attitude and helpful physical posture is a prerequisite to good breathing. Physically the breathing control develops from an area around the waist. The head and body should be balanced, the neck, shoulders and spine should be supported but relaxed, and the rib-cage free to move in and out.

Focusing the sound. We encourage children to focus their sound from a point at about the centre of the forehead so that the brighter end of the voice spectrum is enhanced and singing in tune is made more likely. This releases unwanted strain on the vocal cords and throat and gets rids of harsh and breathy sounds. Singing from the throat is very tiring on the voice and limits the potential range of notes a child will be able to produce with quality.

The sound. Vowels carry the tone and colour of the sound. Well defined vowels enhance the beauty of the vocal sound and project the words more clearly.

Word definition. Consonants give clearer rhythmic definition to our sounds, as well as a clearer understanding of the words. Since most consonants do not carry a pitched sound they are interruptions in the flow of the melody.

▷ The following teaching idea may be used to lay the foundations for those points of technique described on page 157:

To demonstrate, the teacher places both hands, back to back pointing downwards, at a point about the navel and hums a note of comfortable pitch. The hands slide up the wall of the chest to the chin while the teacher continues to hum the same note. The hands then open outwards and away from each other as the mouth is shaped to sing the sound 'mah' (or 'moh') for several seconds. For the children to imitate this, ask them first to open their mouths and the teacher pretends to 'pop in' a 'singing-bean', telling the children that the bean will grow into a singing sound. The children then copy the teacher as the exercise is repeated. The exercise can be varied in duration, pitch, vowel and consonant on subsequent occasions.

When teaching songs

Considerations for the teacher

1 The teacher is the child's model, so use an alert and encouraging posture, and sing with a gentle but positive sound.

2 Know the songs as thoroughly as possible.

3 Try not to use a copy of the song when teaching.

4 Encourage a quiet, focused singing sound; it will aid accuracy of response.

5 Do not expect total assimilation by the children at their first acquaintance with a song. Frequent performing opportunities are preferable.

6 The children should learn both words and melody by rote.

7 As a rule, teach the song before involving other aspects such as actions or a game.

8 If necessary (for teachers in the early stages of experience) use an instrument, e.g. a chime bar, as an aid to finding a suitable starting note.

9 Make clear to the children whose turn it is to sing; this may be done by gesture. Learning a song involves active participation by both teacher and children:

Teacher sings _____	children listen
Children sing _____	teacher listens

▷ It is important for the teacher to resist the temptation to sing with the children. Although sensitive singing with the children can sometimes help confidence in the early learning stages, a teacher's voice is often stronger than a child's voice. Singing with the children can prevent the teacher from hearing accurately the children's response, or prevent the children (child) from hearing their own response. Encouraging the children (child) to respond on their own develops listening skills and confidence.

Teaching the song

1 Sing the song to the children. If they are going to understand the song, it is obviously an advantage to have heard it in its entirety.

2 During the teaching of the song, take opportunities to indicate points of interest, placing the song within a context. The children's interest and attention need to be focused, and this will improve the quality of their response.

3 **a** Sing to the children a phrase of memorable length;
b to the established tempo, the children *immediately* repeat the teacher's phrase;
c repeat the process until they are confident;
d teach the next phrase in the same way and when the point of confidence is reached, sing the first two phrases consecutively, with the children imitating;
e continue this process with succeeding phrases.

4 Through this repetition, encourage:
a a steady tempo;
b rhythmic accuracy;
c melodic accuracy;
d pitch accuracy (good intonation);
e breathing between phrases only.

5 **a** To begin a familiar song, a teacher may indicate the pitch and tempo of the song by singing, for example:

b Experiment with a song by using different starting notes, but always operating within the vocal range of the children.

6 To assist an accurate start:
a assume an alert and encouraging posture;
b make eye contact;
c encourage the children by using appropriate hand gestures and facial expression;
d make an observable intake of breath (one beat, in tempo) before starting.

These suggestions are also useful when requiring a collective start to 'thinking voice' singing.

▷ The teacher needs to listen accurately to the children's singing, constantly assessing the quality of their response.

Movement

Why movement?

There is a strong relationship between music and movement since pulse, rhythm and dynamics originate from muscular activity. A direct experience of these shared elements can be given to the child through the movement of his/her own body. If movement is united with music the child can build up a storehouse of muscular experiences (kinaesthetic memory) which will give meaning to the learning of musical concepts, will enable the child to perform music with an accurate feeling for pulse, tempo and rhythm, and subsequently, will generate ideas for improvising.

The satisfaction a child feels in good rhythmic movement is in itself a source of real aesthetic pleasure.

What movements are appropriate?

1 Movements are chosen for musical criteria. They must offer in movement a true realisation of the musical elements.

2 Movements are drawn from the child's own 'vocabulary' of movement. The child is thus encouraged to move in a natural way.

3 Movements will involve the whole body and activate the large muscle groups as much as possible. (The experience of rhythm is stronger when the whole body moves.)

4 Movements must be chosen which lie within the child's powers of co-ordination. The ability to control weight and larger muscles will play a large part in determining the types of movement performed.

5 In order to extend the range of a child's music/movement experiences, attention should be given to gradually widening and developing the child's powers of co-ordination.

6 Since many movements will involve the whole body, care must be taken to encourage the suppleness and springiness of the weight-carrying joints (hips, knees, ankles, feet, etc.) and to increase the easy movements of all parts of the body (particularly movements of the torso).

Movements involving the whole body

Basic locomotor movements

Walk – a natural, springy walk. Avoid stamping or raising the knees. Only with bare feet can a good rolling use of the foot be achieved, so that a soft, light walk results.

Run – the description 'jog' or 'trot' produces a more controlled run. Keep on the ball of the foot, with short steps.

Gallop – ⁶₈ (compound time). Most children can do this.

Skip – ⁶₈ (compound time). Usually difficult for younger children.

Stride – useful for a slower tempo.

Hop/jump – tends to be exhausting.

Crawl, slide, roll – sometimes useful for limited periods for slow or sustained movements.

Movements performed on the spot

Swing/sway/rock – sitting or standing: ensure these movements flow through the whole body.

Bend, twist, wriggle, shake, curl up, stretch up, or out.

'Work' movements of all types – pulling, pushing, sawing, chopping, sweeping, etc.

Movements using certain parts of the body

With fast or slow tempi children are better able to control movements which use smaller muscles and less weight. The same is true for movements which interpret extracts from rhythm-phrases (rhythm motifs).

Avoid over-use of the arms and encourage the children to move in as varied a way as possible, exploring the movements of all the joints.

Tapping rhythms as 'body percussion' is an important activity but can become very dull unless constantly varied. Encourage hand movements to bounce lightly.

Co-ordination

To achieve a close bond between sound and movement the child must first listen with concentration and then co-ordinate his/her movements in response to what s/he hears.

Good self-control does not imply an inhibited style of movement; on the contrary, it enhances the child's ability to respond well and to move with greater ease and confidence. Developing good co-ordination assists the teacher: music becomes the discipline for the activity of the class.

Stopping and starting

1 In all movement activities the signal for start and stop must be clearly established. It may be:

   a the start and finish of a song;
   b a signal from a percussion instrument, a word, or a certain note;
   c a sung or tapped message such as

Come to me

or

s   d
sit down;

   d determined by the rules of a game.

2 Practise stopping in quick response games. The faster the movement the more difficult it is to control a stop.

3 Vary the signal to encourage keen listening; include two or three different signals in one activity. Avoid too many very abrupt sounds; a quieter signal encourages a tidy, well-controlled stop.

4 Practise a gradual slowing down (rallentando).

Keeping in time

Children have a faster normal speed than adults. Every child has a personal tempo which is determined by size, temperament, health and emotional state. At first the teacher observes and uses the child's natural tempo before asking him/her to conform to one predetermined by the teacher.

1 Ask one child to walk naturally at his/her own pace; the class follows the child's steps with soft taps or quiet singing.

2 Repeat this with other individual children and notice any changes in speed (tempo).

3 Ask two or three children to walk in unison. The class accompanies as before.

4 The tempo having been set by individuals or small groups, the song accompanies their steps until everyone has a secure feeling of 'being in time'.

5 Finally, the children are asked to match their steps to a song tempo given by the teacher.

The children must be given opportunities to practise moving in time in many different ways, so that gradually they learn to adjust their own tempo to a wider range of slower and faster speeds.

Difficulties with keeping in time

There are many reasons why some children have difficulty co-ordinating their movements and keeping in time. These children need more practice of the process outlined above (*Keeping in time* 1–5) by which the music is superimposed on the child's movement. Some children are helped by singing a familiar song with a strong pulse as they move, or by pairing with a child who keeps good time.

Use of space

A whole class of children will need a space large enough for all to move freely, but not to lose contact with the teacher. So that the child's attention is focused on his/her response to the music, the direction in which the child will move and the spaces to be used must be clearly indicated.

1 Aim to use the space fully every lesson.

2 Locomotor movements are at first confined to small numbers of children moving freely, or moving around other children or objects. Larger groups can be asked to move in a straight direction; e.g. side to side, corner to corner.

3 Young children move best as individuals and not in formation or with partners.

4 Specific instructions must be given before the movement begins. The teacher builds up a vocabulary indicating spacing and direction.

The children become increasingly aware of the room and of their movement in relation to others. As their experience and confidence increase they can be allowed to use the space more freely and independently, and to begin to work with a partner.

Changing direction efficiently in locomotor movements is a necessary skill if larger numbers of children are to move freely without collision. It depends on good foot control and is easier if steps are kept small.

The circle

Many singing games require the children to circle, holding hands. Generally, these games are more suitable for 7–8 year olds. The following activities prepare for circle games when the children have experience of walking in time:

a holding hands with a partner while walking (later skipping);

b groups of about eight children practise forming a circle around a hoop or rope, placed on the floor;

c groups of children hold hands in a line and walk or skip along. Stress the twisting of the body when holding hands.

Songs with movement

Always ensure that movements serve a musical purpose, and beware of actions which only illustrate the words. The children's own spontaneous responses when singing often suggest some very good movements.

Add movements only when the song is known and securely sung. Often the teacher, one child, or a group might sing while the others are moving. If the best tempo for movement results in poor diction and intonation in the children's singing of the song, the teacher must provide the song while the class moves.

Non-pitched percussion added to a song can enhance its rhythmic vitality and widen the dynamic range.

Some important teaching points

1 The teacher must learn to **see** if the children are moving in time.

2 Balance vigorous activities with movements of relaxation. Beware of over-exciting or exhausting the children. Movement can release tension and fatigue, and is balanced well by moments of quiet, concentrated singing or listening.

3 Be prepared to move with the children to give them confidence, but the adult must move faster to match the children's tempo. Do not let the children copy your movements.

4 Avoid playing strident percussion sounds with the pulse; they produce a stiff, jerky style of movement.

5 Communicate a sense of pleasure and vitality.

Using instruments

The use of instruments needs to be a feature of the children's musical experiences, together with singing, movement and listening. The *Teaching ideas* in the **Course programme** suggest ways in which instruments can be incorporated into the children's activities.

The use of instruments in these activities is of value because it extends the range of timbres available to children's music-making and the instruments themselves provide a strong medium for reinforcing particular skills and concepts.

Because they are more readily available to schools, the following instruments are particularly appropriate for this course: tambour, tambourine, claves, cymbal, xylophone and chime-bars.

Teachers are encouraged to consider these points:

1 Instruments required for the session should be readily available.

2 The size and weight of instruments should be suitable for young children.

3 How is the instrument best held? It may be necessary for the child to deviate from the usual mode of handling in order to be comfortable.

4 Consider carefully the particular motor-skills required of the child; encourage children to use a supple wrist action rather than a whole-arm action when playing percussion of this kind.

5 Body-tapping and movement activities in general should be seen as an important preliminary stage to the successful acquisition of the necessary motor and aural skills for playing percussion instruments.

6 Children need guidance in discovering the most suitable way to play an instrument; regular opportunities to observe and hear the teacher play are recommended.

7 A selection of beaters with heads of varying textures will augment the range of timbres obtainable from the instruments.

8 When playing the xylophone or similar instrument the children should hold two compatible beaters, one in each hand, and should be encouraged to use the beaters efficiently.

9 Allow time for children to play and experiment with each instrument and to assimilate its particular tone qualities.

10 Encouragement to listen carefully should be given to any child experiencing difficulty in maintaining an ensemble (e.g. accompanying a song). A constant awareness of the musical contribution of others is essential.

11 When planning the purchase of instruments and beaters consider seeking impartial advice. In any case, first try to *hear* the instruments you are interested in buying – the *quality* of sound produced will influence your choice.

12 Avoid subjecting instruments to conditions of high temperatures and humidity. Direct sunlight and extreme dryness will cause wood to warp and rubber to perish.

13 The children's co-ordination skills and imaginative handling will develop *steadily* when instruments are used regularly. But do not allow the use of instruments to dominate your curriculum and its planning.

Listening

Listening programme

Children need to know that milk originates from the cow rather than a bottle; similarly they need to experience live music performance if they are not to form the opinion that music originates from a loudspeaker. Local opportunities to hear suitable live music performance are likely to be limited, but they should be taken or even made – e.g. visiting a theatre or inviting a musician to the school. The child's affective response to music will be greatly enhanced by experiencing live performance, by having an opportunity to see, hear and know the performer through personal contact.

There is also benefit to be gained from listening to recorded music, of course, and the teacher's final choice will depend upon the discs and cassettes to which s/he has ready access.

In choosing which music to present to the class, the teacher is recommended to bear in mind the following points.

1 At this stage, the children's listening span is limited, so each piece should be either short in length or be a short extract (little more than one minute).

2 The music chosen should cover a variety of musical styles, but it is essential that each piece is notable for its quality within that style; it is essential that the children's experience is based upon the best examples.

3 The music should be chosen from the following categories:

   a the written classical tradition;
   b the unwritten, spontaneous folk tradition;
   c music from other countries, in both folk and classical traditions.

4 A variety of performing media should be used. For example:

   a solo vocal (unaccompanied and accompanied);
   b choral;
   c solo instrument;
   d small instrumental ensemble;
   e large instrumental ensemble;
   f electronic instrument(s).

5 Draw the attention of the children to the occasion for which the music is intended (when possible). For example:

   a dance;
   b ceremonies;
   c concerts;
   d advertisements or signature tunes;
   e drama – stories, descriptive uses, musicals/opera.

It is good for the teacher to guide the children's listening by indicating particular features in advance; the choice of listening repertoire might even include examples which relate to the *Skill/Concept index*. However, we should ensure that there are always occasions when music for listening is presented without instruction, so that the children are able simply to hear a piece on its merits, and to accept it on their own terms.

Glossary

The following terms and symbols occur in *Growing with Music: Key Stage 1*:

Words relating to pulse and rhythm

1 Pulse A regular unit of time of audible or inaudible nature.

2 Beat The word used when describing the sensation experienced as pulse. Hence 'the song was 16 beats long' or 'the fourth beat of the bar'.

3 Metre The grouping of pulse into a feeling of stronger and weaker beats. Hence, a regular pattern of beats felt as *strong-weak-weak/strong-weak-weak* produces a metre of 3.

4 Tempo The rate or pace at which the pulse moves.

5 Rhythm A succession of sounds (with or without silences) of variable and/or equal duration moving within a tempo.

6 Rhythm elements The units of note and rest duration. They divide into two categories:

a Simple time – in which the rhythms are associated with the pulse, and its division into *two*.

Rhythm symbol: (one sound) ♩

Rhythm symbol: (two sounds of equal duration) ♫

Rest symbol: (no sound) *z*

b Compound time – in which the rhythms are associated with the pulse, and its division into *three*.

Rhythm symbol: (one sound) ♩.

Rhythm symbol: (three sounds of equal duration) ♫♪

Rest symbol: (no sound) *z*.

7 Rhythm motif
The grouping of several elements.

Written examples: ♫ ♩ (simple)

or ♩. ♫♪ (compound)

8 Rhythm-phrase The grouping of several motifs, analogous to the construction and function of literary sentences.
Written examples:

$\frac{2}{4}$ ♩ ♫ | ♫ ♩ | ♩ ♩ | ♩ *z* ‖

$\frac{6}{8}$ ♩. ♩. | ♫♪ ♩. | ♩. ♫♪ | ♩. *z.* ‖

9 Rhythm names The name given to a rhythm element.

Simple: ♩ = **ta** (pronounced 'tah')

♫ = **ti-ti** (pronounced 'tee-tee')

Compound: ♩. = **tai** (pronounced 'tie')

♫♪ = **ti-ti-ti**

10 Time signature The symbols $\frac{2}{4}$ and $\frac{6}{8}$

The symbol $\frac{2}{4}$ indicates two beats, each of ♩ (**ta**) value, for each complete bar of notation (simple time).

The symbol $\frac{6}{8}$ indicates two beats, each of ♩. (**tai**) value, for each complete bar of notation (compound time).

11 Bar The division of rhythm notation into metre groupings (as confirmed by the time signature).

12 Bar line A vertical line indicating the completion of one bar and the start of the next.

(Example for **10, 11** and **12**):

(The symbol ⊕ on the staff shows the position of **doh** for that particular piece).

Words relating to aspects of pitch

1 Pitch The melodic aspect of a sound. For example, a high sounding melodic note is high in pitch; a low sounding melodic note is low in pitch.

2 Melodic note A single sound of definable pitch.

3 Melodic fragment/motif The rhythmic grouping of several melodic notes. For example:

4 Melodic phrase The grouping of several motifs analogous to the construction and function of literary sentences. For example:

5 Intonation The true and accurate pitch relationship of associated notes. Hence, 'singing in tune' or 'good intonation'.

6 Solfa The singing names of melodic notes. For example: **soh (s), me (m), lah (l)**.

7 Handsigns A series of hand gestures correlated with the solfa names and used for pitch reading. For example:

Other words

1 Improvising The spontaneous shaping of melodic and rhythmic motifs and phrases drawn from previous aural experience.

2 Ostinato A rhythmic (or melodic) motif or phrase, performed repeatedly.

3 Staff/stave The five parallel lines upon which notation is written.

4 Rhythm-solfa A form of melodic notation using solfa symbols in combination with rhythm symbols, written horizontally. This method is used in the *Song collection (rhythm-solfa notation)*.

5 Timbre The tone quality of a voice or instrument.

6 Dynamics The volume of sound.

7 Interval The measured pitch difference between two notes; hence, the upward interval between **doh** and **soh** (e.g. C–G) is described as a **perfect 5th.**

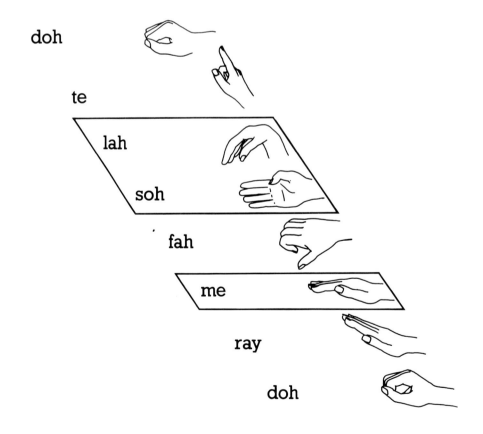

Copymasters

- Although all material in this book is subject to the law of copyright, the copymasters in the list given below may be photocopied according to the needs of the teacher.

  1 The Teacher Planning Chart
  2 Record of Content (1) and (2)
  3 Rhythm Cards (simple time)
  4 Rhythm Cards (compound time)
  5 Reading Sheets
  6 Record of Assessment

- The teacher should decide whether to copy on to card or on to paper. As their name suggests, it is intended that Rhythm Cards be photocopied on to card – or, alternatively, copied on to paper and then pasted on card. They are much easier to use if made of a stiff material. The children might find it helpful if compound time cards were copied on paper of a different colour from simple time cards.

GROWING WITH MUSIC

Teacher planning chart

Class:

Date:

Objective:

Skill/Concept reference	Preparing	Making conscious	Reinforcing	Using in a new situation

Record of content (1)

Class	Teacher

Songs from the Song Collection

Songs A–H	No	✓
A goblin lives in our house	41	
Alice the camel	95	
An elephant goes like this	63	
Apples, peaches, pears and plums	58	
Bells in the steeple	22	
Bought me a cat	77	
Bow, wow, wow!	39	
Button you must wander	82	
Can you tap your fingers?	24	
Chop, chop, choppety chop!	5	
Chuffa, chuffa, chuff!	42	
Clip, clop	50	
Cobbler, cobbler	2	
Cuckoo! Cherry tree	11	
Ding, dong	45	
Down came a lady	84	
Down the hill	48	
Engine, engine	35	
Fair Rosa was a pretty child	88	
Farmer Higgs	94	
Fox is running	76	
Glowing candle-light	53	
Go and tell Aunt Nancy	86	
Hammering here	78	
Hands are cold	73	
Have you seen the muffin man?	96	
Hello, how are you?	1	
Here comes a bluebird	81	
Here I come	67	
Here is the beehive	38	
Here sits the Lord Mayor	60	
Here we go	28	
Hey! Hey! Look at me!	65	
Hickety tickety	43	
High on a leaf	90	
Hush, my dear	52	

Songs I–R	No	✓
I have a dog	32	
I, I, me oh my!	9	
I'm a little Dutchgirl	79	
I see you	21	
I walked to the top of the hill	97	
I wiggle my fingers	64	
Jack-in-the-box	23	
Jelly on a plate	3	
Let us make a ring	68	
Listen, listen, here I come	30	
Little Arabella Miller	31	
Little Johnny dances	56	
Little pony, gallop home	72	
Little Sally Saucer	69	
Lots of rosy apples	33	
Make the porridge in a pan	29	
Mice, mice	4	
My little baby	74	
Oats and beans	87	
Oh, there are four seasons	93	
Once a man fell in a well	51	
One little candle	92	
One potato	7	
Pancake Tuesday	54	
Pears for pies	12	
Pease pudding hot	47	
Pee, Pee, Pollyanna	57	
Piggy on the railway	59	
Pitter patter	49	
Rabbit in the hollow	27	
Rain on the green grass	20	
Rain, rain, go away!	15	
Rap-a tap-a	13	
Rat-a-tat-tat!	71	
Roll up! Here's the fair	19	
Round and round	16	

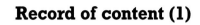

Record of content (1)

Class	Teacher

Songs from the Song Collection – Listening – Project – Other sources

Songs S–Z	No	✔
Sally go round the sun	85	
See my wellingtons	44	
See-saw	10	
See the Indian chief	83	
Sleep, baby, sleep	75	
Snail, snail	14	
Snowman, snowman	40	
Starlight, star bright	80	
Tap, tap, tap!	17	
Teddy Bear, Teddy Bear	66	
Tell me, shepherdess	46	
This is how a drummer-boy/girl	26	
Tick-tack-too	61	
Tick-tock, tick-tock, see my clock	25	
Tick-tock, tick-tock, tell the time	71	
To market	8	
Tom cats, alley cats	36	
Twiddle-di-dee	6	
We're Mother Piggy's piggy piglets	89	
What shall we do?	18	
What shall we play?	91	
Who has the penny?	37	
Who is that I see?	34	
Willum he had seven sons	55	
Zinty tinty	62	

Listening: live music workshops and performances

Projects and topics

Titles from other sources (e.g. carols, songs, hymns)

Listening: recorded music titles

GROWING WITH MUSIC

SMEP — SOMERSET MUSIC EDUCATION PROGRAMME

Record of content (2) Skill/Concept index

Class _____ Teacher _____

No	Skill/Concept index	Observations
1	Finding the voice – class pitch-matching	
2	Finding the voice – individual matching	
3	Developing: a) an awareness of phrase b) a controlled singing tone	
4	Feeling the steady pulse	
5	Distinguishing louder and quieter	
6	Distinguishing faster and slower (tempo). Feeling the pulse internally	
7	Pitch: an awareness of melodic shape	
8	Distinguishing pulse and rhythm	
9	Feeling the rest – aural feature of phrase	
10	Simple time: pattern of two notes to one pulse	
11	Simple time: rhythm names (*ta ti-ti*)	
12	Simple time: rhythm symbols (*ta ti-ti*)	
13	Simple time: sense of metre. Introduction of the bar line	
14	Simple time: the rest symbol z with |	
15	Pitch: distinguishing higher and lower	
16	Pitch: *soh* and *me* with handsigns	
17	Compound time: feeling and recognising compound time patterns (aural)	
18	Pitch: *lah* with handsigns – *l–s–m*	
19	Compound time: three notes to one pulse/names	
20	Identifying and counting melodic phrases	
21	Melody: rhythm-solfa (simple time)	

Rhythm card 1

Rhythm card 2

Rhythm card 3

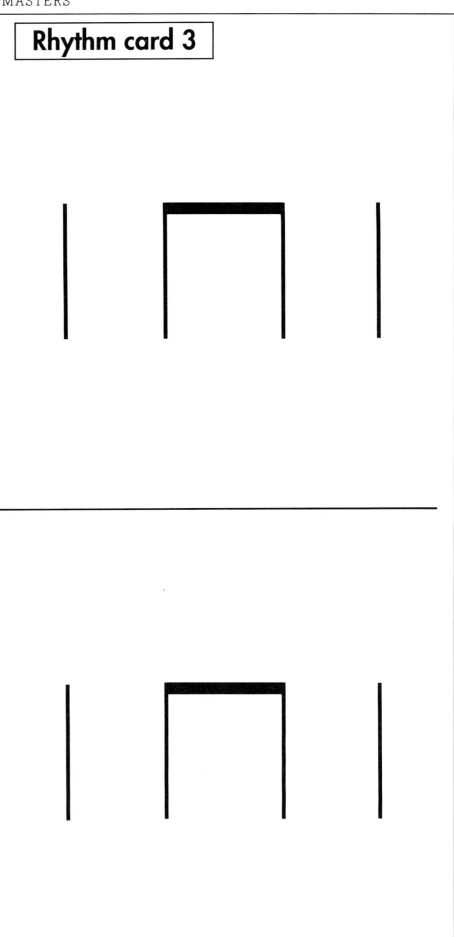

Rhythm card 4

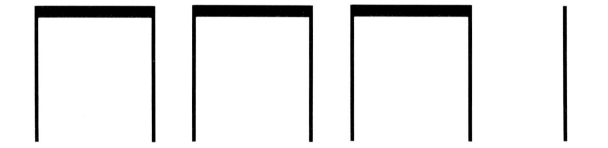

Rhythm card 5

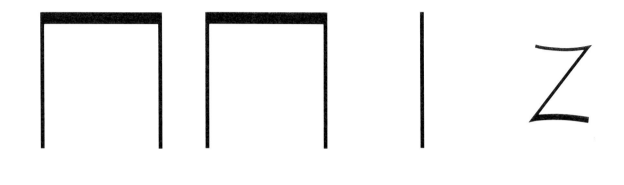

Rhythm card 6

| Z | Z

Rhythm card 7

GROWING WITH MUSIC

SOMERSET MUSIC
EDUCATION PROGRAMME

Rhythm card 8

E | |

E E

Rhythm card 9

Rhythm card 10

Rhythm card 11

E|·

N·

|·

GROWING WITH MUSIC

Reading sheet 1

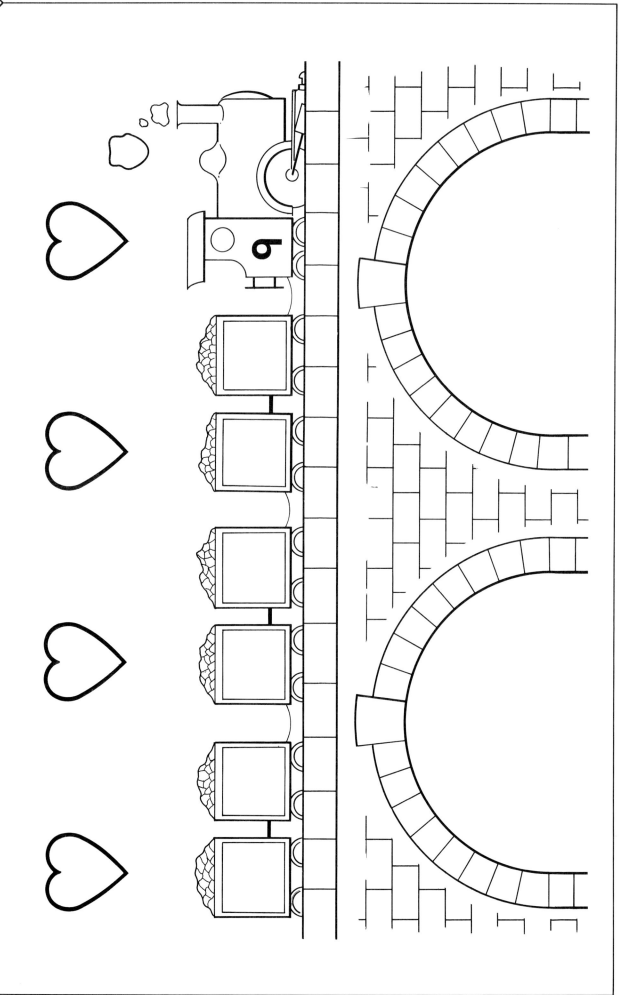

Reading sheet 2

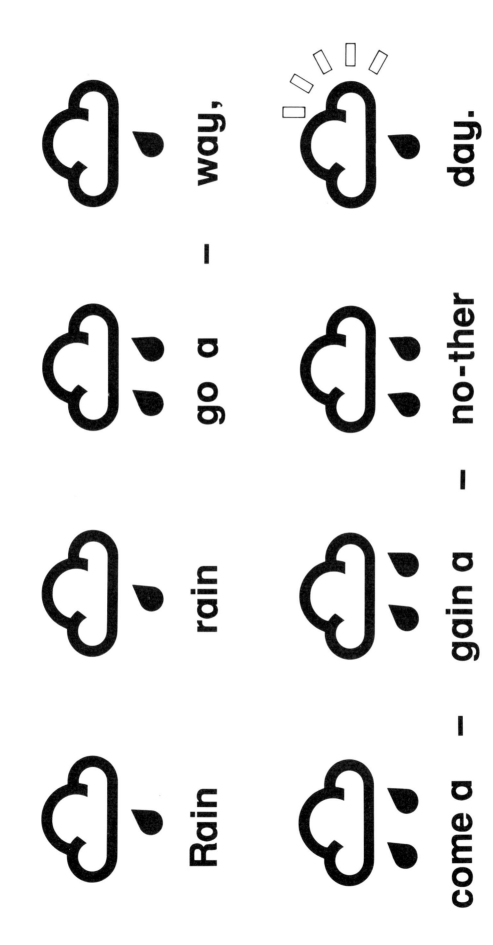

Rain — — — rain — go a — way,

come a — — gain a — — no-ther — day.

GROWING WITH MUSIC

Reading sheet 3

Hey   hey   look at   me

  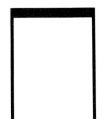

ta   ta   ti – ti   ta

Reading sheet 4

2

clip   **clop**   **clip**   **clop**

off   to   mar - ket   ne - ver stop

GROWING WITH MUSIC

Reading sheet 5

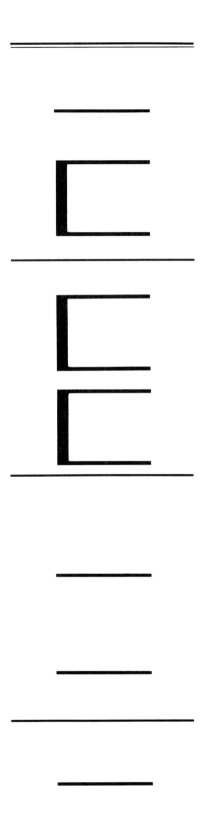

2

Reading sheet 6

2

GROWING WITH MUSIC

Reading sheet 7

2

Reading sheet 8

Glow-ing can-dle –light

 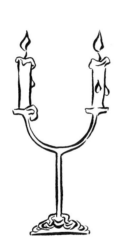  

2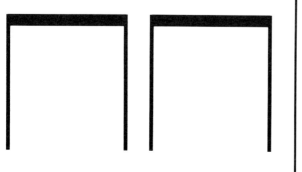

GROWING WITH MUSIC

Reading sheet 9

2

Reading sheet 10

2

GROWING WITH MUSIC

Reading sheet 11

SMEP
SOMERSET MUSIC
EDUCATION PROGRAMME

Reading sheet 12

SMEP
SOMERSET MUSIC
EDUCATION PROGRAMME

Reading sheet 13

2

2

Reading sheet 14

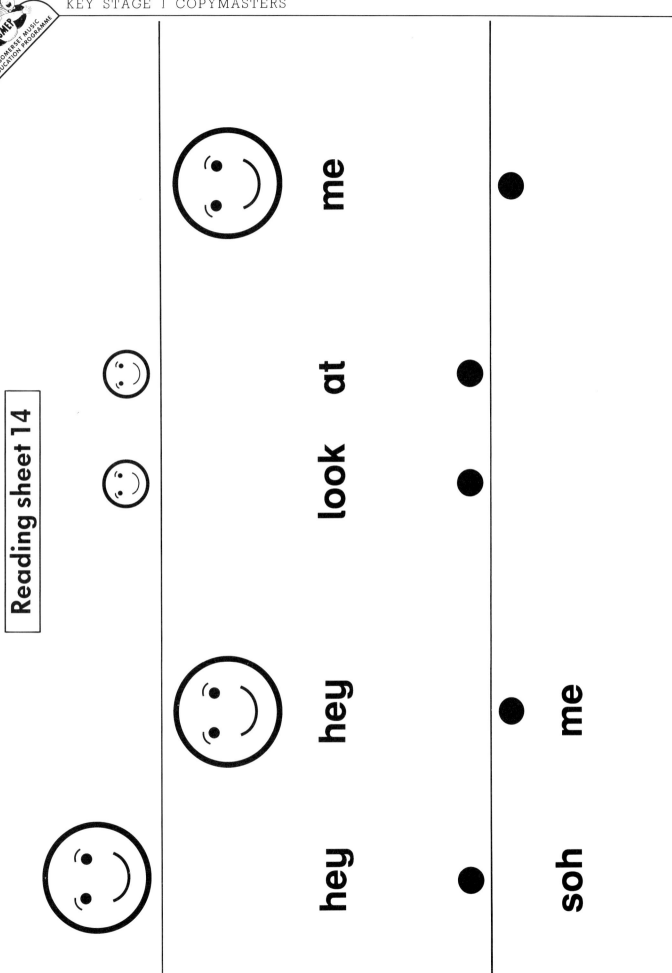

GROWING WITH MUSIC

SOMERSET MUSIC EDUCATION PROGRAMME

Reading sheet 15

Star – light, star bright

s   lah   s   m

Reading sheet 16

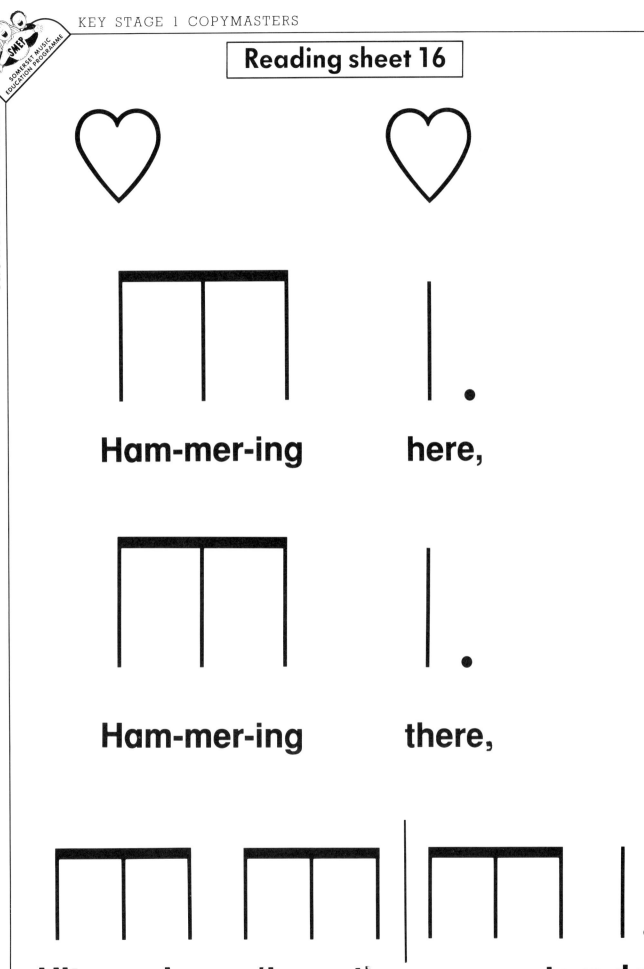

Ham-mer-ing   here,

Ham-mer-ing   there,

Hit   ev - 'ry   nail   as   the   car-pen-ters do.

GROWING WITH MUSIC

Reading sheet 17

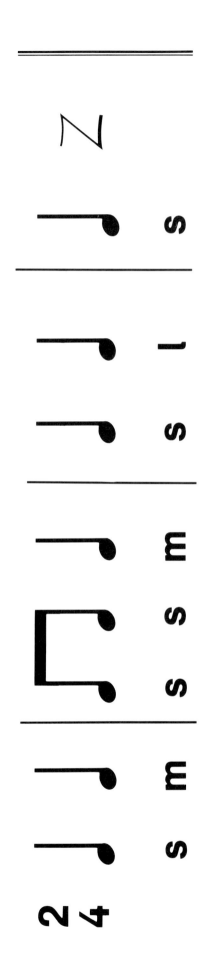

Reading sheet 18

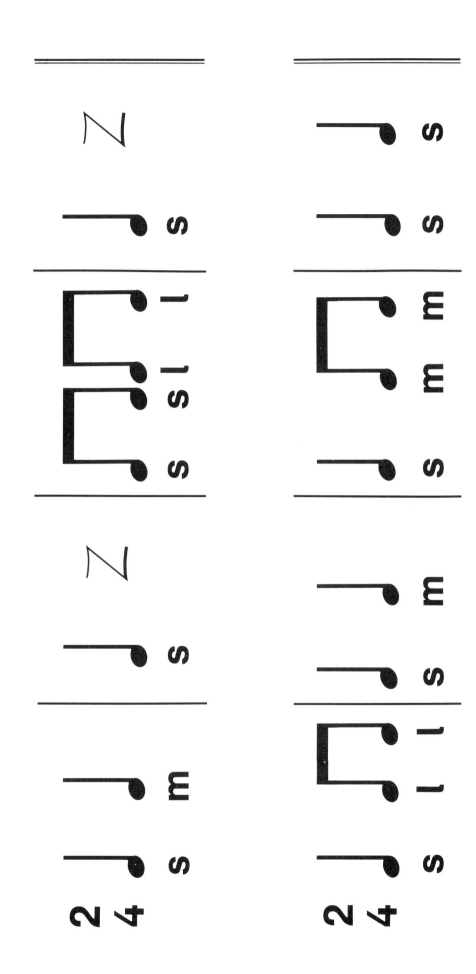

GROWING WITH MUSIC

SMEP — SOMERSET MUSIC EDUCATION PROGRAMME

Class _____   Teacher _____

LISTENING/APPRAISING

- Has internalised musical phrases for subsequent recall and has talked about same/different features in music.
- Has learned to distinguish pulse, rhythm, phrase, pitch and dynamics as basic features of style.

PERFORMING/COMPOSING

- Has memorised rhythm and vocal pitch names and has constructed short rhythm phrases.
- Has improvised short rhythm-phrases and, with the voice, melodic phrases.
- Has found his/her singing voice, has shown control over a variety of body movements.
- Has developed an awareness of pulse, rhythm, tempo, phrase, pitch and dynamics.

Comments

Name

GROWING WITH MUSIC

RECORD OF ASSESSMENT: KEY STAGE 1 (END OF KEY STAGE STATEMENTS)

NC: ENGLAND

Class _____

Teacher _____

SMEP — SOMERSET MUSIC EDUCATION PROGRAMME

LISTENING/APPRAISING

Has talked in simple but appropriate terms about sound and music s/he has made, listened to, performed or composed.

Has listened attentively and has responded to music from different times and cultures and in different styles, and has shown an awareness of differences and similarities.

PERFORMING/COMPOSING

Has recorded his/her own compositions, and has communicated them to others.

Has investigated, chosen and combined sounds to produce simple compositions.

Has sung in a group and has played a variety of simple instruments, demonstrating some control of the sounds made.

Has performed simple rhythmic and melodic patterns by ear and from symbols.

Comments

Name

RECORD OF ASSESSMENT (LEVEL 1)   THE NORTHERN IRELAND CURRICULUM: MUSIC

Class _____   Teacher _____

MAKING MUSIC

Name	Has made sounds for a particular purpose.	Has recognised that sounds may be represented by symbols.	Has joined in singing simple songs.	Has used instruments to accompany singing.	Comments

© Longman Group UK Ltd 1992

Class _____   Teacher _____

RESPONDING TO MUSIC WITH UNDERSTANDING

Has responded to the mood of short pieces of music.

Has responded to sounds in simple ways.

GROWING WITH MUSIC

Name			Comments

SMEP SOMERSET MUSIC EDUCATION PROGRAMME

Class _____   Teacher _____

SOMERSET MUSIC EDUCATION PROGRAMME

MAKING MUSIC

Comments

Has accompanied songs using tuned and untuned instruments.

Has sung a variety of songs as a member of a group.

Has invented symbols to represent sounds.

Has selected sounds in response to a stimulus.

Name

GROWING WITH MUSIC

SMEP
SOMERSET MUSIC
EDUCATION PROGRAMME

Class _____　　　　Teacher _____

RESPONDING TO MUSIC WITH UNDERSTANDING

Has imitated simple, rhythmic patterns.

Has responded to familiar sounds within and beyond the classroom.

Has listened attentively to live and recorded music and expressed his/her thoughts about it.

Comments

Name

Class _____   Teacher _____

SOMERSET MUSIC
EDUCATION PROGRAMME
SMEP

MAKING MUSIC

Name	Has combined sounds in order to express mood and atmosphere	Has invented and interpreted symbols which represent particular sounds or patterns of sound.	Has sung a variety of songs demonstrating some control of the voice.	Has played a tuned or untuned instrument as a member of a group.	Comments

RECORD OF ASSESSMENT (LEVEL 3)

THE NORTHERN IRELAND CURRICULUM: MUSIC

SMEP — SOMERSET MUSIC EDUCATION PROGRAMME

Class _____

Teacher _____

RESPONDING TO MUSIC WITH UNDERSTANDING

Has conveyed, through performance, the style and mood of the music.

Has answered simple rhythmic patterns.

Has listened attentively to live and recorded music and has commented on simple characteristics.

Has discussed sound pictures and patterns composed by him/herself and others.

Comments

Name

© Longman Group UK Ltd 1992

Class _____ Teacher _____

LEVEL A: FIRST ASSESSMENT

- Has begun to identify same/different features in music.
- Has listened to the musical responses of others and has performed in a group.
- Has improvised short rhythm-phrases.
- Has shown control over a variety of body movements.
- Has found his/her singing voice and is beginning to match pitch.
- Has developed an awareness of pulse, tempo and phrase.

Comments

Name

GROWING WITH MUSIC

LEVEL A: ATTAINMENT TARGETS

Class _____   Teacher _____

Has investigated sounds using voices, instruments and everyday objects, recognising differences and contrasts between musical sound and noise.

Has demonstrated some control in pitch and rhythm; has shown ability to memorise simple songs containing repetitive melodic and rhythmic patterns.

Has demonstrated abilities in such basic playing techniques as shaking and tapping, keeping the beat and repeating simple rhythm patterns.

Has selected appropriate sound sources and combine and link sounds to convey effect in a short invention.

Has worked co-operatively with others and has presented and performed music to the teacher and other audiences.

Has identified sound sources; has responded to music of a clearly identifiable character, sensing pulse and speed; has recognised the melodies of songs already learned.

Name

Comments

RECORD OF ASSESSMENT: KEY STAGE 1 (FIRST ASSESSMENT)   NC: WALES

Class _____   Teacher _____

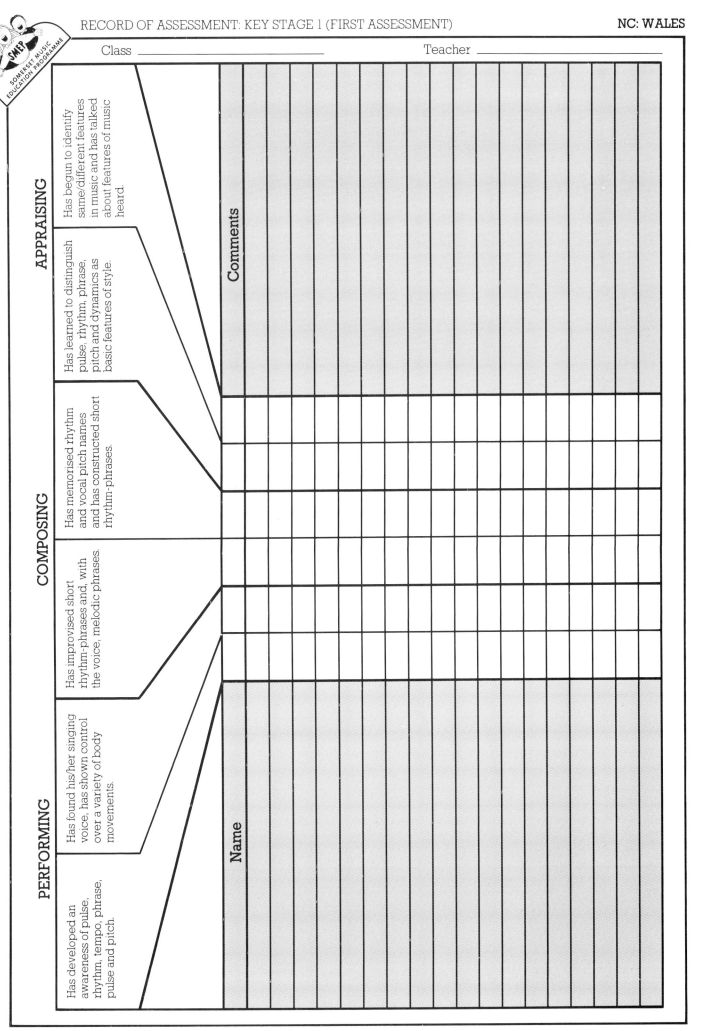

APPRAISING

Has begun to identify same/different features in music and has talked about features of music heard.

Has learned to distinguish pulse, rhythm, phrase, pitch and dynamics as basic features of style.

COMPOSING

Has memorised rhythm and vocal pitch names and has constructed short rhythm-phrases.

Has improvised short rhythm-phrases and, with the voice, melodic phrases.

PERFORMING

Has found his/her singing voice, has shown control over a variety of body movements.

Has developed an awareness of pulse, rhythm, tempo, phrase, pulse and pitch.

Comments

Name

GROWING WITH MUSIC

RECORD OF ASSESSMENT: KEY STAGE 1 (END OF KEY STAGE STATEMENTS)

NC: WALES

Class _____   Teacher _____

APPRAISING

Has talked about sounds and music s/he has listened to, performed and composed.

Has listened attentively to a variety of music and has recognised and responded to its main elements.

Comments

COMPOSING

Has stored his/her music for subsequent recall, using appropriate means to communicate it to others.

Has investigated, chosen and combined sounds to produce simple compositions.

PERFORMING

Has sung in a group and has played simple instruments, demonstrating some control of the sounds made.

Has performed simple rhythmic and melodic patterns by ear and from symbols.

Name

Appendix

- The following pages link the 'Growing with Music' programme to Programmes of Study for England, Northern Ireland, Scotland and Wales. A detailed chart is provided for each country showing how 'Growing with Music' connects with these statutory requirements at Key Stage 1.

'Growing with Music' in relation to
National Curriculum Programmes of Study (England)

PROGRAMME OF STUDY ITEM	'GROWING WITH MUSIC'
Pupils should:	**Observations and examples from the Programme:**
Memorise and internalise short musical patterns and simple songs, and imitate and recall simple rhythms and melodies.	Memory is basic to the learning process in music. It is the foundation of musical thinking (e.g. recalling, comparing). Use of memory is developed consistently throughout the Programme.
Read simple signs and symbols and perform from them.	The Programme requires that pupils read and perform from conventional rhythm symbols and solfa pitch symbols/signs: *S/C 11, 12, 14, 16, 19, 21.*
Sing a variety of simple unison songs with some control of breathing, dynamics and pitch.	The song collection of 98 songs is chosen for the Key Stage 1 age-range to serve the needs of children's aural/vocal development: *S/C 3 and notes in the Teacher's Book.*
Develop the technical skills needed to control the sounds of a range of tuned and untuned instruments, through playing simple pieces and accompaniments.	At this Key Stage, instruments are introduced not only to provide a range of sound textures, but mainly when they are the most effective means for reinforcing acquired concepts: *S/C 7, 8, 13, 14, 17, 19.*
Practise and rehearse, responding to direction.	This is a constant feature of the Programme, using the song collection of 98 songs.
Share their music-making, presenting performances effectively to different audiences, for different purposes, and in a number of places with different acoustics.	The Programme offers opportunities for pupils to perform as individuals, with partners, as a group, and as a class – to the teacher, to each other and outside the class or school.
Take part in simple vocal and instrumental improvisations, compositions and arrangements.	Improvising is a strong feature within the Programme's systems of learning; it is essential that pupils improvise with newly-acquired concepts in new situations, and as a basis for composing.
Explore and use a range of sound sources including their voices, bodies, sounds from the environment and instruments, tuned and untuned.	Without denying the value of other sound sources, this Programme is largely based upon the use of the voice because of the significance of the child producing the sound themselves.
Create, select and organise sounds in response to different stimuli.	The pupil's awareness of basic music elements and his/her ability to distinguish between them is the foundation upon which musical progression takes place: *S/C 3, 4, 5, 6, 12, 17, 19, 20, 21.*
Communicate simple musical ideas.	It is a constant feature in this Programme that pupils work as a class, in groups and individually to perform with voice and instruments, and to analyse, evaluate and discuss their music ideas.
Use and understand simple signs and symbols for musical sounds when composing.	At Key Stage 1, most activity is based upon music activity and working with newly-acquired skills. Signs and symbols are used to reinforce this music experience: *S/C 11, 12, 14, 16, 19, 21.*
Record their own compositions.	The Programme offers many opportunities for pupils to record the results of their composing.

(S/C = Skill/Concept)

'Growing with Music' in relation to National Curriculum Programmes of Study (England)

KEY STAGE 1

PROGRAMME OF STUDY ITEM	GROWING WITH MUSIC
Learn to listen with care and concentration to their own and other's music, and make broad distinctions within main musical elements.	The Programme uses a repertoire based on children's songs, from which basic music skills and concepts are acquired: *S/C 3, 4, 5, 6, 7, 8, 10, 12, 15, 16, 18.*
Listen to, discover, make, compare and talk about everyday sounds of all kinds.	The Programme uses voice and instruments to perform musical sounds. Other sound sources can also be used, provided that the sound made is appropriate.
Respond to the musical elements, character and mood of a piece of music by means of movement and other forms of expression.	Pupils work with basic structural and expressive elements of music, using voice, movement and instruments: *S/C 3, 4, 5, 8, 9, 13, 15, 20.*
Listen to and talk about a variety of live and recorded music exhibiting contrasts of style, including works by well-known composers and performers as well as their own and others' compositions and improvisations.	The sharing of musical experiences and outcomes is a feature of this Programme. The pupils develop the skills and vocabulary needed to assess and evaluate their musical experiences.
Discuss how sounds and rhythms are used in music to achieve particular effects, and learn to recognise some different characteristics in music from different times and places.	The musical examples within the Programme are taken from a variety of times and cultures. The Skill/Concept index is concerned with those elements of music which are common to all styles.

(S/C = Skill/Concept)

'Growing with Music' in relation to National Curriculum Programmes of Study (NORTHERN IRELAND)

KEY STAGE 1

PROGRAMME OF STUDY ITEM	'GROWING WITH MUSIC'
Pupils should have opportunities to:	**Observations and examples from the Programme:**
Explore ways of making sounds.	Without denying the value of other sound sources, this Programme is largely based upon the use of the voice because of the significance of the child producing the sound themselves.
Experiment with sound sources to discover their wider possibilities.	In addition to discovering sound sources, the pupils discover their voices and how to control the sound they make.
Listen to sounds and find simple ways of describing them.	The Programme helps pupils to develop quickly a basic vocabulary of musical terms through their experience with sound.
Recognise and identify familiar sounds and differences between similar sounds.	Distinguishing between 'same' and 'different' within musical elements is a feature of this Programme.
Recognise, discuss and classify remembered sound.	With partners, pupils work with the sounds and musical features they have recognised and identified, using these in new situations.
Recognise differences in quality of sound and tone colour.	This occurs mainly through the use of percussion instruments, particularly when working with more than one part.
Imitate, recall and answer simple rhythmic and melodic patterns.	Memory is basic to the learning process in music. It is the foundation of musical thinking (e.g. recalling, comparing). Use of memory is developed consistently throughout the Programme.
Develop an awareness of pulse.	A feeling for pulse is introduced at the beginning of the Programme, since it is the basis for understanding all aspects of rhythm, beat, metre and tempo.
Develop an awareness of rhythm and pitch.	The Programme uses a repertoire based on children's songs, from which many basic music skills and concepts are acquired: *S/C 3, 4, 5, 6, 7, 8, 10, 12, 15, 16, 18.*
Recognise the following musical concepts: duration, pace, dynamics, pitch, texture, silence.	The pupil's awareness of basic music elements and his/her ability to distinguish between them is the foundation upon which musical progression takes place: *S/C 3, 4, 5, 6, 12, 17, 19, 20, 21.*
Select sounds to create simple sound pictures in response to stimuli such as pictures, stories and poems.	Improvising is a strong feature within the Programme's systems of learning; it is essential that pupils improvise with newly-acquired concepts in new situations, and as a basis for composing.
Control sound and silence to create short musical pieces.	Pupils work with basic structural and expressive elements of music, using voice, movement and instruments: *S/C 3, 4, 5, 8, 9, 13, 15, 20.*
Accept and offer suggestions about their own and others' sound pictures and patterns.	The sharing of musical experiences and outcomes is a feature of this Programme. The pupils develop the skills and vocabulary needed to assess and evaluate their musical experiences.
See music in print and be aware that sounds can be represented by symbols.	Pupils are encouraged to develop the capability to read and write musical symbols as representations of their aural experience. In this way, notation always has meaning.

(S/C = Skill/Concept)

'Growing with Music' in relation to National Curriculum Programmes of Study (NORTHERN IRELAND)

KEY STAGE 1

PROGRAMME OF STUDY ITEM	'GROWING WITH MUSIC'
Pupils should have opportunities to:	**Observations and examples from the Programme:**
Find ways of representing and interpreting sounds and sound patterns using graphic or traditional symbols.	The Programme offers many opportunities for pupils to record the results of their composing.
Join in simple songs, using action or movement as appropriate.	This is a constant feature of the Programme, using the song collection of 98 songs.
Sing a variety of simple songs, developing some control of breathing, dynamics and pitch.	The song collection of 98 songs is chosen for the Key Stage 1 age-range to serve the needs of children's aural/vocal development: *S/C 3 and notes in the Teacher's Book.*
Perform songs in keeping with the style and mood of the words.	The Programme uses voice and instruments to perform musical sounds. Other sound sources can also be used, provided that the sound made is appropriate to musical development.
Play tuned and untuned classroom instruments alone and with others.	At this stage, instruments are introduced not only to provide a range of sound textures, but mainly when they are the most effective means for reinforcing acquired concepts: *S/C 7, 8, 13, 14, 17, 19.*
Accompany songs using available instruments.	The Programme offers opportunities for pupils to perform as individuals, with partners, as a group, and as a class – to the teacher, to each other and outside the class or school.
Listen to live and recorded music and respond to its musical elements, mood and character.	Learning activities are based upon whole class and group work. Music-making, using songs from the song collection and instruments with specific tasks constantly demand listening to others.
Comment on simple features and characteristics of music.	It is a constant feature in this Programme that pupils work as a class, in groups and individually to perform with voice and instruments, and to analyse, evaluate and discuss their music ideas.
Express preferences.	Within the Programme, pupils are constantly evaluating musical experiences and outcomes.

(S/C = Skill/Concept)

'Growing with Music' in relation to
Music Curriculum and Assessment policy in Scotland

PROGRAMMES OF STUDY STRANDS	'GROWING WITH MUSIC'
Summary of Levels A – D	**Observations and examples from the Programme:**
Investigating and exploring sound A Sounds in the environment. Contrasts of sound. B Exploring wider range of sounds and sound quality. C Mood in music. Obtaining subtle effects. D Experimenting. Electronic sound sources and computer programs. Simple acoustics.	The Programme is based upon a Skill/Concept index for which a sequence of skills, concepts and musical features have been carefully selected. These include features relating to mood, texture and expressiveness, encouraging their use in appropriate ways for the inventing activities of the pupils. Notations are used which primarily enable and support music thinking processes.
Using the voice A Acquiring a song repertoire. Pitching in vocal range. B Developing vocal control. Songs from many cultures. C Singing with greater expression. Beginning two-parts. D Wider range of styles. More complex work in parts. Improvements to the quality of vocal sound. Breathing.	The Programme is based upon use of the voice and associated aural development. It shows how children need to find their voices before they are seven if they are to grow in confidence and self-esteem. Internalised musical thinking is a natural consequence of using the voice as a medium of musical expression because the child makes the sound and controls the way it is used. The programme is based upon a song collection of 253 songs, all carefully chosen for their suitability for particular age-ranges.
Using instruments A Learning to manipulate and care for instruments. B Showing control of speed and dynamics. Techniques. C Playing by ear, from parts and with expression. D Practising more complex parts. Improving fluency and reaching higher levels of achievement.	A range of tuned and untuned instruments are recommended for use with this Programme. Instruments are first introduced not only to provide a range of sound textures, but mainly as an effective means of reinforcing acquired concepts. Instruments are used increasingly throughout the Programme to a point at which graded instrument ensemble material is achieved (scores and parts are provided as Copymasters). Graded choral music is also included in Copymaster form (Teacher's Book 2B).
Creating and designing A Inventing supported by the teacher. B Sound pictures. Recording and notation systems. C Short inventions to convey mood. Structure. D Composing, inventing and arranging. Structure. Inventing music for specific occasions.	The teaching programme in the Teacher's Book and the cooperative activities within the Pupil's Books regularly require pupils to respond to a variety of stimuli, including verse, stories, 'moods', specific occasions, drama and dance. Composing is a strong feature throughout and many opportunities to present performances of work done are suggested.
Communicating and presenting A/B/C/D Working cooperatively and showing respect for the opinions of others. Taking turns and accepting 'group responsibility'. Sharing performance with a variety of audiences and for a variety of occasions. Communicating with others through music whenever possible.	It is a constant feature that pupils work as a class, in groups and individually to perform with voice and instruments, and to analyse, evaluate and discuss musical ideas. The Pupil's Books, a valuable resource for Level B, frequently require the pupils to work with partners, sharing tasks, taking turns and exchanging activities, so that essential communication and group responsibility takes place as a result.
Observing, listening, reflecting, describing and responding A Listening to sounds around. Stories/movement. B Short extracts. Expressing preferences. C Identifying genres. Discussing preferences. D Wide range of styles and genres. Live performance. Making and accepting criticism of musical structure and performance.	The song collection and musical examples used in the Programme provide a rich repertoire of music from all continents of the world, including Scottish and Gaelic tradition. The Teacher's Book frequently gives background information about the material and its origins, as well as guidance on listening to recorded music. It also includes musical examples from different periods in European history.

(S/C = Skill/Concept)

'Growing with Music' in relation to National Curriculum Programmes of Study (Wales)	KEY STAGE 1

PROGRAMME OF STUDY ITEM	'GROWING WITH MUSIC'
Pupils should be **taught** how to:	Observations and examples from the Programme:
Memorise and internalise short musical patterns and simple songs, and imitate and recall simple rhythms and melodies; perform a short musical pattern, responding to simple symbols.	Memory is basic to the learning process in music. It is the foundation of musical thinking (e.g. recalling, comparing). Use of memory is developed consistently throughout the Programme.
Sing a variety of simple unison songs with some control of breathing, dynamics and pitch.	The song collection of 98 songs is chosen for the Key Stage 1 age-range to serve the needs of children's aural/vocal development: *S/C 3 and notes in the Teacher's Book*
Develop the technical skills needed to control the sounds of a range of tuned and untuned instruments, through playing simple pieces and accompaniments.	At this Key Stage, instruments are introduced not only to provide a range of sound textures, but mainly when they are the most effective means for reinforcing acquired concepts: *S/C 7, 8, 13, 14, 17, 19.*
Practise and rehearse, responding to direction.	This is a constant feature of the Programme, using the song collection of 98 songs.
Sing songs and play instruments in a group, maintaining an accurate pulse and developing the ability to listen to other performers.	Learning activities are based upon whole class and group work. Music-making, using songs from the song collection and instruments with specific tasks constantly demand listening to others.
Share their music-making with others, presenting performances effectively.	The Programme offers opportunities for pupils to perform as individuals, with partners, as a group, and as a class – to the teacher, to each other and outside the class or school.
Explore and use a range of sound sources including their voices, bodies, sounds from the environment and instruments, tuned and untuned.	Without denying the value of other sound sources, this Programme is largely based upon the use of the voice because of the significance of the child producing the sound themselves.
Take part in simple vocal and instrumental improvisations, compositions and arrangements.	Improvising is a strong feature within the Programme's systems of learning; it is essential that pupils improvise with newly-acquired concepts in new situations, and as a basis for composing.
Create, select and organise sounds in response to different stimuli.	The pupil's awareness of basic music elements and his/her ability to distinguish between them is the foundation upon which musical progression takes place: *S/C 3, 4, 5, 6, 12, 17, 19, 20, 21.*
Record their own compositions; memorise, internalise and recall music which they have created.	The Programme offers many opportunities for pupils to record the results of their composing.
Communicate simple musical ideas.	It is a constant feature in this Programme that pupils work as a class, in groups and individually to perform with voice and instruments, and to analyse, evaluate and discuss their music ideas.
Listen attentively to their own and other's music, in order to recognise and make broad distinctions within main musical elements.	The Programme uses a repertoire based on children's songs, from which basic music skills and concepts are acquired: *S/C 3, 4, 5, 6, 7, 8, 10, 12, 15, 16, 18.*

(S/C = Skill/Concept)

'Growing with Music' in relation to
National Curriculum Programmes of Study (Wales)

**KEY
STAGE
1**

PROGRAMME OF STUDY ITEM	'GROWING WITH MUSIC'
Pupils should be **taught** how to:	Observations and examples from the Programme:
Identify sounds in the environment and in the classroom, including sounds made by classroom instruments.	The Programme uses voice and instruments to perform musical sounds. Other sound sources can also be used, provided that the sound made is appropriate to musical development.
Respond to the musical elements, character and mood of a range of music by means of movement and other forms of expression.	Pupils work with basic structural and expressive elements of music, using voice, movement and instruments: S/C 3, 4, 5, 8, 9, 13, 15, 20.
Listen attentively to, respond to, and talk about live and recorded music of a variety of styles, times and cultures.	Because of the teaching and learning styles encouraged by this Programme, the pupils are constantly evaluating musical experiences and outcomes.
Evaluate their own and others' work.	The sharing of musical experiences and outcomes is a feature of this Programme. The pupils develop the skills and vocabulary needed to assess and evaluate their musical experiences.

(S/C = Skill/Concept)

Acknowledgements

Designed by Heather Richards and Mick Harris.
Illustrated by Hardlines and Paul Howard.
Cover illustration by Ian Newsham.
Edited by Stephen Attmore.

We are grateful to the following copyright holders for permission to reproduce songs and music:

The Author, Richard Addison for 'Here we go' & 'Little pony gallop home' from *Play and Sing*; A & C Black for 'Tick Tock Too' by Ruth Sansom & 'High on a by Clive Samson from *Rythm Rhymes* ed. Ruth Samson; Boosey & Hawkes Music Publishers Ltd for 'I, I, me oh my' from *Be a Real Musician* by G Russell-Smith. © Copyright 1977 by Boosey & Hawkes Music Publishers Ltd, 'Bells in the Steeple', 'Roll up here's the fiar', 'Glowing Candle light' from *The Kodály Way* by C Vajda. © Copyright 1974 by Boosey & Hawkes Music Publishers Ltd, 'Bow wow wow', 'Here comes a Bluebird' from *150 American Folk Songs* by P Erdei. © Copyright 1974 by Boosey & Hawkes Inc, 'Engine, Engine' from *Let's Sing Together* by D Bacon. © Copyright 1973 by Boosey & Hawkes Inc, 'See my Wellingtons', 'Who is that I see?' from *50 Nursery Songs* by Z Kodály. © Copyright 1970 by Boosey & Hawkes Music Publishers Ltd; Chester Music London/ Music Sales on behalf of J Curwen & Son for an extract from 'Tom Cats, Alley Cats' by Anne Mendoza from *Seven Simple Songs for Children*. Copyright © J Curwen & Sons Ltd, 8/9 Frith Street, London WIV 5TZ; Dover Publications Inc for 'Hickety tickety' from *Traditional Games of England Scotland and Ireland* by A Gomme; Harrap Ltd for 'I wiggle my Fingers' by Linda Chesterman from *Music for the Nursery School*; Hertfordshire County Council for 'Here is the beehive', 'Rat a tat tat', 'Snowman Snowman' from a collection of materials for teachers compiled by Hertfordshire LEA Primary music Specialists; International Music Publications for 'Down the Hill' by Ann Mendoza. © EMI United Partnership/IMP; International Music Publications/ CPP/Belwin Inc. for 'Button you must wander' from *JUST FIVE – PLUS TWO, A Collection of Pentatonic Scales* by Robert E Kersey. © EMI united Partnership/ IMP. U.S Copyright © 1972 by Bellwin-Mills Publishing Corp. c/o CPP/Belwin Inc, Miami, FL 33014. International Copyright Secured. Made in USA. All Rights Reserved; the Author, Winifred S MacLachlan for 'See the Indian Chief (originally 'Indians') from *Music Activities for Retarded Children* by David R Ginglend and Winifred S MacLachlan; Macmillans, London for 'Tick tock tell the time true' by Mona Swann from *Trippingly on the Tongue*; Alison McMorland for her arrangements of 'Cuckoo, cherry tree', 'Fair Rosa', 'Pee pee Polyanna' collected & arranged in *The Funny Family*, published by Ward Lock Educational. Copyright Alison McMorland, 'Hush my dear' collected & arranged in *Brown Bread and Butter*, published by Ward Lock Educational. Copyright Alison McMorland; Novello & Co Ltd for 'Once a Man Fell in a Well' translated & set by Anne Mendoza from *Graded Rounds for Recorders* Book 1; Oxford University Press for 'Farmer Higgs', 'Go and Tell Aunt Nancy' from *Oxford School Music Book* (Junior Part 1) by R Fiske & J P B Dobbs, 'Clip Clop', 'I See You', 'Pitter Patter' from *Oxford School Music Book* (Infant) by J P B Dobbs & R Firth, 'We're Mother Piggy's piggy piglets' from *Oxford School Music Book* (Beginners Book 3) by G Reynolds, 'Let us make a ring' from *Clarendon Book of Children's Songs*, 'My Little Baby' from *Sociable Songs* (Book 1A) by A Mendoza, 'The Children's Band' from *More Songs for Music Time* by Mabel Wilson, 'Here sits the Lord Mayor' from *Oxford Nursery Rhyme Book (N.B.)* by Opie, 'Pancake Tuesday' words by F Wood from *Sixty Songs for Little Children*; Oxford University Press/Editions Durand S A Paris/United Music Publishers fro 'Tell me Shepherdess' in *A Third Sixty Songs for Little Children* by Wiseman & Northcote (arrangement)/*L'Anthologie Populaires Français* by Joseph Cantaloube (Melody); Random Century Group for 'I Walked to the top of the Hill' from *Over and Over Again* by Barbara Ireson & Christopher Rowe; Schott & Co Ltd for 'Fox is running', 'Hands are cold', 'What shall we do' from *Perry Merry Dixy* by J. Horton. © Schott & Co London; Verlag Carl Ueberreuter for 'Es war eine Mutter, die hatte vier Kinder' ('Oh, there are four seasons') from *Das Gross Buch Der Kinderlieder*. © by Annette Betz Verlag, Vienna-Munich; Unwin Hayman and the Authors, for 'A Goblin lives in our House' by R Addison from *Play and Sing* 1, 'Chop chop choppety chop' by Rodney Bennett from *First Steps in Speech Training*; the Author, Terence Woodhouse for 'Lots of Rosy Apples' (words and music).

We have unfortunately been unable to trace the copyright holders of 'Little Johnny Dances' from *Music Activities with Young Children* by J Gilbert; 'Listen, Listen'; words to verses 1 & 2 of 'Make the Porridge'; 'Rap-a tap-a'; 'Tap, tap, tap'; 'Chuffa, Chuffa, Chuff'; 'I have a dog'; 'Jack in the box'; 'Mice, Mice' by S. Vickery; 'Hammering Here' by A Kingston; 'Round and Round' & 'See-Saw' in *The Kodály Method* by L. Choksy; and 'Can you tap your fingers?' by Margaret O'Shea, and would appreciate any information which would enable us to do so.

Longman Group UK Limited
Longman House, Burnt Mill, Harlow, Essex CM20 2JE, England and Associated Companies throughout the World.

© Longman Group UK Limited 1992

First published 1992
Second impression 1993
ISBN 0 582 03937 1

Set in 10½/12½ pt Rockwell Light (Linotron)
Produced by Longman Singapore Publishers Pte Ltd
Printed in Singapore

The publisher's policy is to use paper manufactured from sustainable forests.